or a small church. He
new 'mindskin' so that ⟶
Town Mega Church!

The church Gary is talking about is not a Christian fellowship or a community church. Gary is talking about a large, influential church *for* the community. A church that influences all spheres of a community.

After all, these days you grow a church by growing the community."

Dr. Ed Delph
Founder and President of Nation Strategy
Phoenix, Arizona, USA

"The attitudes and leadership principles taught in *The Small Town Mega Church,* when adopted by pastors and their leaders, could change the dynamics of church in the small community. This is a book pastors and leaders in smaller communities should read."

Mel C. Mullen
Foundering Pastor, Word of Life Centre Church and Ministries
Red Deer, Alberta, Canada

The Small Town

MEGA

CHURCH

Foreword by Dr. Pat Francis

Pastor Gary W. Carter

THE SMALL TOWN MEGA CHURCH

Scripture quotations marked NKJV are taken from the New King James Version / Thomas Nelson Publishers, Nashville: Thomas Nelson Publishers. Copyright © 1982. Used by permission. All rights reserved. Scripture quotations marked MSG are taken from The Message. Copyright © Eugene H. Peterson. Published by NavPress, Colorado Springs, Colorado, in association with Alive Communications, Colorado Springs, Colorado. Scripture quotations marked NIV are taken from the Holy Bible, New International Version. Copyright © 1973, 1978, 1984 by International Bible Society. Used by permission of Zondervan Publishing House.

ISBN-13: 978-1-926676-90-6

Printed in Canada.

Printed by Word Alive Press
131 Cordite Road, Winnipeg, MB R3W 1S1
www.wordalivepress.ca

WORD ALIVE PRESS
Just Write!

Dedicated to my best friend and wife Kim, for walking with me all these years. We have been on an incredible adventure for over thirty-five years and I have never had to walk alone!

To our kids, for holding on to us when things where hard, for choosing to see the best in us and believing in the call of God on our lives. I love you all!

To Randy and Joan, for over twenty years of friendship, fun and patience. You carried us through many tough spots in our journey.

To Gail, for always being there to get us through.

To our staff in all locations, for their daily hard work and sacrifice.

To our teams, for carrying so much responsibility.
To our church, who has "loved us through" our weaknesses.

To all who have made us so strong.

This book is not about what we have learned, it's about what we have lived!

Thank you.

FOREWORD

God has decreed that power and influence shall be the spiritual DNA and manifestation of His Church. His purpose was clearly shown in Ephesians 3:10: *"His intent was that now, through the church, the manifold wisdom of God should be made known to the rulers and authorities in the heavenly realms"* (NIV). This means that through His Church, God intends to rule and exercise dominion both in the natural and in the spiritual, in heaven and on earth, and in societies, communities, and nations.

In this book, Apostle Gary Carter speaks from the experience of one who is the founding apostle of a small town mega church in Drayton Valley, Alberta. In visiting his Church, I was impressed by both his and the Church's influence in many spheres of society such as government, economics, education, and media… to mention a few.

A small town mega church is one that is committed to influencing its community with programs and events for societal transformation. The reality of Church growth is that most Churches in North America, if not the world, have a membership of less than five hundred. This can be due to many factors such as the size, culture, location, and religious competition in a community.

The good news is that more important than the size of a Church is its positive impact in transforming lives and influencing its community. In this book, readers will find practical insights and training on how to lead successful Churches for greater impact. Regardless of the size and membership of a Church, all Churches need to have a mindset for societal transformation and impact. A mega mindset should be the reality of all Church leaders because we serve a "Mega God."

As you study about the core values and liberating structures of strong Churches, you will get the opportunity for self-examination and also to reexamine the structure, systems, and processes of local Churches for change and enhancement for future growth and impact.

Pastors will be taught on how to raise up and train great leaders with a broader knowledge of church responsibilities and with a mega mindset. In the words of Apostle Gary, "Our future churches will manage well if they are well managed! Our number one goal is to facilitate success." Well said.

The Church of Jesus Christ is the solution for the world. We have the power and anointing of Jesus Christ, who is building His Church regardless of spiritual and natural opposition throughout the ages.

God loves the world. This book is a must-read for all Pastors who are serious about developing strong Churches for greater impact, influence, and infusion into societies, communities, and nations. The kingdoms of this world shall become the kingdoms of our Lord Jesus Christ as He reigns through His powerful Mega Church.

PAT FRANCIS, PH.D.

Pat Francis Ministries

www.patfrancis.org

TABLE OF CONTENTS

Foreword   ix

Introduction   1

ONE   The Small Town Mega Church Mandate   7

TWO   What Is It and What Does It Look Like?   13

THREE   The Mega Church Mindset   24

FOUR   The Leader's Perspective   39

FIVE   Vision Needs Values   52

SIX   Liberating Structures That Activate and Empower   84

SEVEN   The Training Ladder: Pastors in Training Program   91

EIGHT   Preparing Your Teams   96

NINE   Overcoming Growth Plateaus   111

TEN   Joining Strength and Wisdom   134

ELEVEN   The Trends I See   137

TWELVE   Creating Internal Cultures   160

THIRTEEN   Breaking the Cycles of Average   172

FOURTEEN   Building Momentum   179

FIFTEEN   Mobilizing Marketplace Ministries   191

SIXTEEN   Final Thoughts   199

Statement of Faith   205

Other Resources and Book Available   208

INTRODUCTION

This book was inspired from one of our staff meetings as we were trying to identify why our churches continue to grow. We were attempting to identify and focus on our main strengths to use for a marketing and branding initiative. The problem was, we couldn't determine any one area that stood out in our strengths. We seemed to be equally gifted and have similar strength in all departments and ages. We looked at the emphasis of the various seasons over the fourteen years of our journey and found we could not identify growth trends or direct cause and effect patterns. Even with all of this information, stats, and reports in front of us, we still were not able to see any one thing that stood out that we felt made us unique. This was encouraging and disheartening all at the same time. We were encouraged that we seemed to have a great balance in all departments and ages. We have been and still continue to be consistent in our growth patterns, management styles, and core values... or any other gauge of success we could discuss. The disheartenment came from not being able to put any one thing on a poster or tagline that defined or even came close to reflecting what the Lord has done in our church.

One afternoon, I was sitting in my office with our multimedia/marketing director and we took another stab at trying to define our identity or create an all-inclusive tagline that we could use in our marketing. In the course of discussion with our staff, I stumbled upon a phrase that I feel is a perfect reflection of our identity. Our discussion led away from "what" we do, on to "how" we do things. As we talked about the procedures and ways of our church, we looked at the leadership focus, corporate team dynamics, service flow, facility development, marketing, staffing positions, teams we have created, and influence the Lord has given us in our community, and I said we don't function like a small town church... we function like a mega church! We are a small town mega church!

In the days to follow, we became more aware of our uniqueness and our strengths expressed in the concept of a small town mega church. From this perspective, we once again discussed our programs, leadership structures, procedures, financial management, training programs, and every other thing we could think of and it became obvious that our strength is found in "how" we do things, not in the "what"!

The vast majority of churches in North America, and even in most of the world, are small churches. These are churches of fifty to two hundred and fifty people. I also hear stats of the high number of pastors that leave the ministry every month in North America, and it saddens my soul. Our staff listens to the hurts of other pastors who have poured their lives into a church and have yet to experience the growth they anticipated. At times we almost feel guilty that we don't generally have leadership problems. We continue to grow without evangelism (in the traditional sense, at least) and our lives are full of blessings. We asked ourselves, *What are we doing that makes this thing work? Why do people come to our church? What brings them, and then why do they stay?* and many other similar questions. Through a lot of thought, discussion and prayer, I believe we have identified the main strategies, structures and ways that make our church a successful small town mega church!

We believe that this is our branding identity. It is the core of what the Lord has created us to be. Our intention is to share our experiences with other leaders of small churches to bring encouragement, inspire some new ideas, explain some of our strategies, and impart our success with as many as we can. If you are a pastor or leader in a small church but you have big dreams, you are probably a good candidate for a small town mega church. If your vision seems too large for your city or if everyone around you is laughing at the size of your dream… you are reading the right book! I have always taught our team, "If people aren't laughing at the size of your vision, it isn't big enough!" We need to be developing a God-sized vision for our lives and our churches. A God-sized vision will seem impossible to the natural man, but we know that we serve the God of the impossible! What we thought was impossible fourteen years ago has become our present reality. The impossible can become yours too, if you have the courage to keep going forward, the discipline to develop skills, and the determination to live your dream!

There are many reasons why a church doesn't grow and I know we won't solve all of them in one book, but we must start somewhere! I have attended many church growth conferences hosting some of the best speakers in the world. Many of them refer to a small church as a church of five to seven hundred people. Most pastors can only dream of having a solid five hundred in their church. The conference speakers and authors are accurate in their stories, skilled in their strategies, and blessed in their success, but it is out of reach of the majority of small town churches, or small churches within a city. We hear about their marketing strategies, but in a small church there is no budget to even begin. They tell us the importance of having excellent worship that will draw in the next generation, when we only have one organ or accordion player in the church. Some don't even have that much, and are forced to sing along with CDs (which may be a better idea than the accordion anyway!). In a small church, it seems there is never any money to get anything done. The facilities are inadequate for activities and we are forced to rely entirely on volunteers who are willing, but many times unable, to run the programs of the church. The pastor becomes the jack of all trades, but hasn't the time to be the master of one. They eventually get overloaded and burned out.

Hard work is important while building anything, and the ministry is no different. But hard work in itself can only grow the church until the pastors' time and energy is used up. At the point where the leaders' or team's success becomes larger than he or they can manage, it forces them to incompetence. They are not bad people, lazy, wrong spirited, or misguided in their intentions. Their efforts bring them to a place of change, but they are stuck in an overwhelming busy routine. In an attempt to keep up with the demand, they work harder within their present leadership dynamics, structures, and programs. The structures and programs worked to get them to their present level of success. The problem is that the very thing that got them to this level of success has become the limiting factor for continued growth. We have tracked our progress from the beginning of the church. We started out with about eight people in a living room, and now we are reaching about three hundred and fifty in a community of under seven thousand. We have also branched out into two other communities in the region, we plan to plant our fourth church in the area very soon, and we are growing a church we planted in the nation of Belize. We are also in our sixth season with our Interns Bible School and our young people have built a recording studio. They have put out their first CD, called "Freedom!".[1] Our marketplace ministry is growing and the church is getting stronger each year. We continue to see many people give their lives to the Lord, families get restored, and the blessings of God released into their lives.

For such a small church in rural Alberta, Canada, our successes are obvious, but I am not putting them into this book to boast. Our boast is in the Lord! Our goal is to encourage everyone that is trying to build a great church in a smaller community. It can be done! We did it and you can, too! But *you will be faced with change*. There isn't any way of avoiding the changes that are needed to grow from fifty people to two hundred and fifty, and beyond. There are leadership roles, relationships, and responsibilities that need to be changed. The pastor's role changes the most! There are plateaus created by leadership availability, financial strength, facility space, program development, and many other elements of success we will discuss in this book. We are passionate about your success and it is our intention to develop resource materials and mentor leaders in

---

[1] "Freedom!" can be ordered online at www.life-church.ca

every way possible to become a small town mega church!

If you are a pastor that has already passed the attendance mark of six or seven hundred, you will find much of what we are teaching to be familiar. You wouldn't be where you are if you didn't understand some of the principles we will propose in this book. You may be giving different names or putting different expressions to the principles, but the basics of successful church growth remain.

I know the principles presented in this book work for large churches as well. I have taught most of this material in mega churches in many cultures around the world over the last few years and it has been received as great insight into mid-sized and mega church environments alike. Our passion is directed at pastors and leaders of small churches who are not only willing to continue working, but to work smarter—not harder. I am writing this book to those who are looking for new small town church growth ideas and proven strategies, to those who are crying out to the Lord for someone to walk with them into the success they know they can achieve. If you are saying "Amen"... or, "Hey, that's me!"... then welcome to the teaching of Life Church International's small town mega church!

ONE

THE SMALL TOWN MEGA CHURCH MANDATE

I believe we need to start our journey with an end in mind. I heard a preacher once say that the Lord ran up to the end to come back to the beginning to lead us to the end. I agree! I see the mandate of a church in Genesis 1:28.

"Then God blessed them, and God said to them, 'Be fruitful and multiply; fill the earth and subdue it; have dominion over the fish of the sea, over the birds of the air, and over every living thing that moves on the earth.'" (Genesis 1:28, NKJV)

The Message Bible states it this way: *"God blessed them: 'Prosper! Reproduce! Fill Earth! Take charge! Be responsible for fish in the sea and birds in the air, for every living thing that moves on the face of*

Earth.'" (Genesis 1:28, MSG)

When I read this passage, I believe we have a mandate from God to do a number of things. First: position ourselves to receive God's blessings. This positioning is about our relationship with the Lord, the unity of the body, the obedience of our lives, our attitudes, and our perspective of applied faith. How we see ourselves is how the world will see us and what will determine the size of our God. We can contain or limit God by the smallness of our faith and the narrowness of our perspective. When we come before God, we need to be obedient to follow what we do not yet know or fully understand and open enough to explore possibilities beyond our personal experience. This becomes very important as we integrate the next generation. The values of the Christian life are consistent throughout the generations, but the expression of our faith is ever changing. We can very easily position ourselves so strong in what was that we miss what is and limit what could be.

Secondly, He said to be fruitful, or to prosper! This comes as a command, not a suggestion or a goal to achieve. It is part of the mandate of God to be fruitful. Everything we put our hand to should increase. The Bible says we can have an abundance for every good work. So why are we so short of finances all the time? We identified at least three areas of possibility.

1. God is holding out on us. This is not likely in light of the cross.
2. The devil is blocking or robbing our blessings. This has legitimate possibility, but I refuse to allow him to get my attention or to cause me to think like a victim, so I ignore as much of his noise

as I can.

3. The third option is the most likely, and it is found in our ability. In a parable in the New Testament, a man gave out talents according to the ability of his servants (see Matthew 25:15). This shows me some principles of increase. I can trust God, I have the authority to deal with the devil, and I can develop the skills I need to bring increase into our church. This last one is totally in my control. I hope for supernatural help, I fight the devil everyday, but I work as hard as I can to improve our corporate capacity and my own personal skills. The increase in our church has been directly related to individual leadership development which increases corporate capacity.

The third element in the mandate is the law of multiplication. When the Lord gives us a revelation, we need to move from "revelation" to "proclamation." When we proclaim the revelation, we are moving into an act of faith. An example of this would be in receiving a revelation from the Lord or an inspiration to take an offering in the church. As I proclaim the revelation, I am stepping out in faith, but as the money comes into my hand, I no longer need faith, as I now have a tangible product in my hand produced by revelation, proclamation, and an act of faith. Now I need to ask the Lord for wisdom. My act of faith has given me some seed. Now I need to get the wisdom of God so I can sow the seed or use the seed for something that increases or multiplies my life and/or fills the ministry need.

We tend to give as we are moved with compassion, and it isn't wrong, but giving from compassion in itself doesn't necessarily multiply our lives. There is a big difference between giving out of compassion or obedience and the principle of sowing a seed to reap a harvest. We should give to the poor, but we can also sow to increase! Ultimately, we need to know what the Lord wants us to sow into. Giving all of your offering to the poor is right, if the Lord has told you to give it to the poor. Building an orphanage is right, if the Lord told you to do it. Giving to the youth is right, if God said so. Sowing finances to build a church to equip the saints is also right, if that's what the Lord has told you to do. Sowing into some-one's life to build a business to provide many jobs or to finance Gods kingdom is just as right, if that's what the Lord told you to do. The point is this: the key to multiplication is obedience to the wisdom of God, not just random acts of faith in themselves. That is why I believe in the principle of tithing to the local church. I give to the local church because it multiplies back much more to my life than I could ever put in.

The mandate goes on to say that we are to take charge of the earth. We could get caught up in a power trip if we were to take this instruction wrong. The world is looking for answers, and we have them. We may not understand the answers yet—it may take some prayer, some work, and some discussion to find them—but they are there. The unsolved never-ending challenges the world faces are ongoing opportunities for your church to take charge. What can our God do about that problem? What does He say and how do we communicate His instructions without sounding like we are judging and condemning those it is meant to help? Taking charge is about taking responsibility for our city. What can we do about the housing, the lost jobs, the economic future, the crime rate, or family development? We start by being willing to take charge. This happens first before God as we come before Him with a willing heart to be an ambassador for the King in our city. We can then report for service to the leaders of the city with humility, and hopefully some credible suggestions addressing their problems. The issues we face while trying to engage church and state, or church and marketplace, are issues of credibility. Many times we are not being realistic, or are uninformed or too self-centered to be credible. When we are credible, the city is quite willing to let us take charge. Through the process of credible engagement, we can saturate society with kingdom principles and create an atmosphere of faith and interest in our God.

The last issue in the mandate is dominion. We are to have dominion, or authority, over all the earth. This is an issue of responsibility. Only those who will take responsibility will walk in God-given authority. As we take responsibility for our city, God starts to release the authority we need in order to address the spiritual climate. We wrestle not against flesh and blood, but against principalities and powers in heavenly places (see Ephesians 6:12)

Our battle is not with man. True spiritual authority is not meant to be used towards man. Spiritual authority is to win the war in the heavenlies. The only entity on earth that has the authority to deal with the powers of darkness is the local church. Our mandate is the same as it was for Jesus, to destroy the works of the devil. This means winning the battle by prayer for our schools, businesses, politicians, families, and justice systems. A battle won in the spiritual realm will manifest itself in the natural realm. We take responsibility in the natural realm, but exercise dominion authority in the spiritual. The invisible will move the visible! This is covered in more detail in my book, *The Power to Effect Change.*[2]

---

[2] *The Power to Effect Change* is available to order from www.life-church.ca

TWO

WHAT IS IT AND WHAT DOES IT LOOK LIKE?

We all know of the mega churches throughout the world. I am writing this book poolside on the beach of Waikiki in Honolulu, Hawaii. We are here to attend a leadership conference with some great church leaders from many nations of the world. One of the speakers spoke about his organization of over a million members. Wow! Many at the conference have churches larger than my whole city! But there is more to a mega church than just size. A mega church has a "presence" in a city. I recently heard it described in comparison to an aircraft carrier. I was told that when some of the smaller nations of the world get into tensions, and war becomes a possibility, the American Navy can send an aircraft carrier into the region, parking just off the coast but remaining in international waters. They don't have to do anything but sit there. The presence of the strike force power on that ship causes those who are threatening and promoting conflict to reconsider their actions.

This is a great parallel to a mega church presence in your city. We desire to build such strong churches in the cities and nations of the world that their mere presence will cause city or national leaders to reconsider social policies and not initiate a battle with the strike force power of the local church.

We have achieved a mega church presence in our community and are on our way to reproducing it in other cities as well. A mega church presence is achieved when its attendance hits five percent of a city's population. In a community of five thousand, you will hit a mega church presence at about two hundred to two hundred and fifty people. A city of ten thousand needs a church of five hundred to achieve a mega church presence. At twenty thousand, you need approximately one thousand in attendance, and so on. When a mega church presence is achieved, you have a great cross-section of culture, diverse giftings, and the sector influence to have a voice in almost any community shaping activity. Politicians recognize two powers. One is the power of wealth and the other is the power of mass. They need economic support to be effective, but they also need the voting mass to agree with their leadership and keep them in power. Reaching a small town mega church status gives you enough influence in both spheres to be a significant part of shaping the future well-being of your city.

The local church is the greatest anchor for our cities and nations. It is the epicentre of social reform, the magnetic north of the social conscience, the greatest place of social integration. Local churches are called to be the builders of our society's moral fibre. The local church is intended to be the model of healthy society and the equipping centre for all the pillars of the community. There are many opinions of how many pillars or key areas of strength make up a functioning society. I use eight. They are:

1. Governance
2. Economical
3. Social Programming and Care
4. Environmental (in the fullest meaning, this represents the stewardship of all things for the next generation)
5. Cultural Identity
6. Education
7. Infrastructure
8. Faith

A mega church presence in a city of any size must have an awareness and strategic plan to engage and align these pillars with kingdom principles.

A mega church has a responsibility before God to care for its city. We say, "Pastor your city and the church will grow as a by-product." To whom much is given, much is required. With great success comes great responsibility. A smaller church can serve some needs in a community, but it doesn't usually have the resources, manpower, and in many circumstances the expertise to lead a city. As a church grows and matures, many of these limiting factors are removed and a church can have a real and tangible leadership presence and expression in the city. The local church should be at a battle ready stance at all times. Ready to do battle *for* their city, not against it!

We have bought into the idea that city government doesn't want any connection between church and state. Although this may be true in some cities, and it certainly has a truth on some issues in every city, it shouldn't be seen as a blanket truth with every city or every issue. While I was a city councillor, I saw how the issues of our community looked from the other side of the bench. The problems are complex and the resources are limited. The normal or accepted procedure of city leaders is to engage the community with discussion groups in the hopes that someone can and will come up with an idea on how to overcome the challenges of affordable housing, rising taxes, job loss, or reduced economic development. They are aware of the failure of most of our present social systems in reducing crime rates or relieving social tensions. City leaders are not lazy, stupid, or out of touch. They are, however, only human and most have very little experience dealing with such complex problems. Many are wage earners who are nonetheless expected to make budgeting choices with millions of tax dollars. Most of them just take the advice of the city managers or consultants until a consensus is reached. The problem is that a consensus can be reached by the uninformed and inexperienced and end up being very wrong.

There are many ways that cities try to educate their leaders, but the turnover rate is very high and the education tends to stay at entry level as new leaders are elected. The church should not be silent! This is an opportunity for us to engage our cities, present credible options, and help to develop our culture. At our church, we are currently building up a group for business owners, and one of the roles they will play in city leadership is to engage the process of city budgeting. We can and should ask questions, get clarification, and use our mass influence to bring attention to some economic issues. If we go into town halls with our forty-pound Bibles and an attitude, we may be heard, but we will never be embraced. I believe the Lord will give us economic strategies to build healthy communities if we will make ourselves available and engage the process.

The whole concept of city governance is about engaging the community. Our city officials are elected and hired to serve our collective well-being. One of the hardest challenges for any politician is getting an audience with positive feedback and creative brainstorming. When I was in city government, there were many issues we advertised seeking public feedback only to find a very small crowd turn out to make their voices heard—and many of those voices had some kind of axe to grind with the city. After a few public sessions, I saw that the same people were showing up for every discussion. They were the interested citizens, but they did not represent a true cross-section of society. What if the church invited the politicians to some feedback and brainstorming sessions? A mega church should have a cross-section of culture meeting at least once a week. The feedback from that mass of people can be very helpful to city leaders. The problem has been in the past that churches tend to take, not give, to their communities. They tend to fight against and not *for* them, only addressing the issues that affect their cause, not the well-being of society as a whole. We are called to be the head... so let's engage!

The church is the best networking system in the world. During the time I served in politics, it was amazing to see how many times an issue came up for which I knew someone I could call or bring in to provide us some ideas. Any city can network very quickly anywhere in the world if they make connections through a local church. The real problem of separation of church and state comes from our side of the table. We want to make the initiative somehow about our church, or some other self-serving value, instead of just serving the strength and well-being of the city at large.

The church is also a great place to activate and inform our citizens about social change. Most of the cities in North America would have twenty to forty percent of their population base influenced directly, or relatively directly, through the faith community. That is a huge mass of voter strength. The politicians know about it during the election season, but stray away from engaging the mass as soon as they get their seat. I don't believe it's out of intentional exclusion. I believe it has more to do with our lack of engagement in the issues they are facing. In a recent example, a city of a million people in our country advertized for nearly a year to establish what they called "round table discussion groups" to address city issues and provide feedback to the leaders. They were seeking feedback from social, economic, environmental, and cultural sectors. I was in that city speaking to about sixty pastors who were on a strategic journey to influence their city for Jesus. I asked them how many had joined the round table discussions. No one had. I then asked how many even knew about the round table discussion groups. No one had! The sad news was that even after they realized the government was almost begging them to come and take part, no one to my knowledge ever did. This is the real issue. The local church has disengaged itself from the community. We are not involved in anything that is beyond the four walls of the church. We have become self-serving and yet we want the community to come to us. In the great commission, Jesus told us to go forth into all the world! Let's engage!

There are not many city leaders who will seek out the ministerial sector to get economic advice, because we are not seen as the experts of that field. But when they are trying to address social issues, they very much see the church as seasoned in the care and communication to people of all ages. As a small town mega church, this represents one of our greatest opportunities to lead, serve, and shape our community. The advantage of a small town mega church is that we also have the volunteer base and the programs to get involved in family crises, whether it be through early intervention or making ourselves available for post-crises care. The local church has great potential to provide excellent long-term follow-up. It can be done in cooperation with the social service agencies of your city. When we interact with city officials from this perspective, and with this kind of intention, they embrace the church with open arms. These are some of the reasons I believe bigger is better for the local church.

A pastor once said, "When you see a need, if you have nothing, you can do nothing; if you have a little, you can do a little; and if you have a lot, you can make a difference! Wealth creation is not about money. It's about effective living." A small church is consumed with survival, and in many cases has no financial or leadership capacity to address city problems. A mega church becomes more cost effective and has more discretionary income. The larger and better managed a small town mega church is determines the magnitude of difference it can make.

A small town mega church is defined as a church that has become large enough to be an obvious presence in the city it's in. Due to their size, they have a considerable mass of volunteers. We have experienced many times for ourselves, and heard similar testimonies from other churches, how they have served their city with volunteers and made their events a huge success. A small town mega church has in its membership the expertise and financial strength to engage the community with enough wisdom and resources to make a difference.

A small town mega church has a responsibility to be the model or example of a healthy society. We represent a true cross-section of our city, with all its strengths and weaknesses. We are also a real representation of all the social challenges our city faces. In the nation of Canada, where I live, we are seeing immigration increasing annually. We have an accepting attitude towards all people. This is a positive trait of Canadian people, but it also can be the very thing that causes some of our greatest social tensions. Many of the people groups that come to Canada come here to find a new life, but work very hard to keep their former lives intact—complete with cultural values, beliefs, and lifestyles they thought they were leaving behind. The only real difference is one of geography. I'm not presuming to know these people's motivations, and I realize that freedom, economic opportunity, and even health care can draw people to a new nation. The point in this context is this: we as a culture need to become experts at integrating new people into our society. When we are dealing with the immigration process of a few people, the task seems manageable, but as the numbers begin to be counted in the thousands, we are not just adding to the challenges; they increase exponentially. Many issues of social integration are very complex, because like us, people are very diverse... even those from the same cultural background. *Integration in a shrinking global economy is the number one social challenge of the twenty-first century.*

In the past, we faced the combining of age, color, sex, and social status. Now we are faced with language issues, faith issues, or issues of unfamiliar cultural dynamics. The influx of diverse people groups is reaching a critical mass. There are enough people from other cultures of the world arriving in Canada and the United States today to influence the economic and social fabric of our cities and nations. The main social challenge of the next fifty years will be to integrate those of mixed faith and cultures into our communities. Any collective culture that doesn't integrate will segregate, and a segregated culture is divided against itself and will not stand. It decreases the collective well-being of society and reduces its economic strength.

This integration challenge is another ideal opportunity for the small town mega church. We have the diversity of people, skills, and environments to be a catalyst for integration. Economic strength may attract people to a region, but only social engagement will keep them. It is good economics for a city to have a healthy faith community embracing its newcomers into a positive, relational environment. Churches such as these provide people with an immediate sense of belonging.

Over the years, the local church has been seen as a hospital of sorts for the socially wounded. We do play an important role in that area of society, but it shouldn't be our only identity—nor our greatest one! An engaged and effective small town mega church moves from the unique primary identity of being a hospital for the weak to being influential as an embassy for our King! An embassy in a foreign land has the ability to make a difference. An embassy is made up of representatives of another nation in a foreign land. The local church should be taking on that role for Jesus. We are to be a place of safety, strength, influence, and authority, a place that has the authority and resources to make a difference.

These are some of the reasons why I believe we should strive to build mega churches! I don't believe any church is too big. There are many churches of all sizes that have lost their passion to transform their cities, but that doesn't mean that transformation can't still take place. Our passion for Life Church International is to partner with, build, and provide resources to leaders who have a similar desire to build small town mega churches. A city of any size will recognize and respect the critical mass of any church that has reached a significant percentage of their population and has the resources, management skills, and determination to make a difference. When you reach that critical mass and strength in proportion to your population base, you have just joined the ranks of a true small town mega church.

OKAY! I'M IN! HOW DO I BUILD ONE?

The motivation for writing this book was to work with those who feel called to a community that may not be the largest city in a region, or to a region of a city that has not produced much fruit. I am not going to give you strategies of how to build a church of five or fifteen thousand people. I will leave that to people who have far more insight than I do.

If a church of five to ten thousand is your goal, and you are already past the one thousand mark and on your way to greater success, listen to people like Pastor Rick Warren, or the many others who have gone before you. You will find great wisdom for your church and city from their insights, and God bless you as you do. But if you are like me and feel called to smaller communities and the big city mega church strategies seem too far out of reach for your budget and membership strength... I have good news for you! You too can become a small town mega church. Your church can have enough critical mass and strength to make a difference. Big city mega church strategies may not fit your budget or manpower capacity, but the strategies of the small town mega church can be used by organizations of any size. I have travelled to many nations to train and teach leaders in corporate team dynamics in the local church,[3] so I know the principles of the small town mega church (or, as we have come to call it, the STMC) remain relevant to big city churches as well. While it remains relevant and will work in larger settings, that is not our target audience. Our passion is to help small churches implement some strategies to enjoy a mega church presence in a smaller community. In order to have the same per capita mega church presence we have in our community, a church in a city of one million people would need to have fifty-five thousand members. You can have unlimited influence with a small church if you refuse to be limited by small church thinking. You can do small church in a big way! Let's take a look at how it's done.

---

[3] Visit our website for more information on these training courses.

THREE

THE MEGA CHURCH MINDSET

Success starts in our minds. The Bible says that as a man thinks in his heart, so is he (see Proverbs 23:7). This is a proven principle in every dimension of life. The greatest limitation of a small church is its mindset or its thought processes and perspectives. Like the people in the Bible days of Joshua and Caleb, we can limit our success simply by what we see. Most small churches can only see the giants in the land and it stops them from even trying to possess the possibilities God sets before them. This perspective will keep a church small and limited in its influence.

But there are some who will have the ability to see the grapes! Those will become an STMC. We need to see the possibilities and refuse to be overcome by fear and small thinking. During the days of Joshua and Caleb, the people saw themselves as grasshoppers—so others saw them as grasshoppers (see Numbers 13:33). *The first step to becoming a small town mega church is in believing you can be one.* Many pastors tell me that they feel called to a small church. Many Christians say they prefer small churches because they are more intimate and personal. We have to decide up front if we *are* or *are not* going to be a mega church. What size is big enough? A church will not grow beyond your vision! You must ask, "Is it the will of God for us, or not?" A church will not surpass your faith. Your faith will determine your reality. Your faith will control your actions. Ask yourself, "Am I willing to do what it takes, or am I just doing my job?"

If you said you *are* going to be a mega church, the bigger the better, and that you will not limit God with what you can see in the natural, you are forming a mega church mindset. You may be the smallest tribe, in the smallest city, in an unknown land, but so was King Saul (see 1 Samuel 9:21). What about the shepherd boy David who became king? He started out as someone who seemed to be a nobody and appeared unimportant to everyone; even his own family didn't see anything significant, but look how God used him! He may have been the youngest of his family, only a shepherd boy, but he was a shepherd boy with a destiny! Say to God, "I am willing to do whatever it takes to be all I can be!"

If you are still with me, you are on your way to becoming a mega church. Start to see it by faith! What does it look like to you? Who will run it? How will the services flow? There is an endless stream of questions to answer. The small town mega church training and resource materials will guide you through the process and allow you to break growth barriers, increase your influence, and bring enjoyment to the journey.

In my book, *The Power to Effect Change*,[4] I state that we should *pastor our cities, and our churches will grow as a by-product.* I still believe this is the place to start. A church that is defined by four walls will limit itself to relative smallness in its city. Our church isn't defined by its four walls. It is defined by the effectiveness of our ministry to the community. Many city-reaching strategies others have developed are based on meeting the needs of a city. I am certainly not against meeting needs, but it shouldn't be all we do. I think of it this way: If there were one hundred individuals who had need and you had one hundred thousand dollars, you could give each one a thousand dollars and meet their need for a short season of time. Eventually the money would be gone and the need would return. It helps, but it doesn't solve the problem. This is similar to the traditional approach churches apply to missions. A STMG approach is to meet the immediate need in a way that can eventually become self-supporting.

I started to think about Jesus as He lifted the loaves and fishes up to God and saw it multiply to meet the needs of five thousand. The needs of our cities are opportunities for the church to be creative. What if we took the resources available—in this illustration, one hundred thousand dollars—and gave it to one or two who had the ability to build a company that could employ the other ninety-eight? If we succeeded, we could meet the immediate need and in the process create a loaves and fishes self-supporting, sustainable plan. This kind of thinking moves us from a small church mindset to a mega church mindset.

---

[4] Available at our website, www.life-church.ca

We tend to think that if we are small, we can't make a difference. The reality is that your biggest problem isn't the size of your church; the real problem is the size of your creative leadership ability to address the needs and wants of your city in a sustainable way. Think beyond your walls. Embrace leaders who don't attend your church, or any other church for that matter. Catch a vision beyond your own limitations and position yourself for greatness beyond your means.

I believe God was up to something when our city was first created. I call this the "redemptive purpose." The body of Christ needs to identify and serve the redemptive purpose, or the reason God created our city in the first place. Every city has inherent unique strengths. When we identify them and determine why the Lord has given these special strengths to our region, we can build a church that facilitates the city's success. As we serve the redemptive purpose for our city, we can bring every sector into alignment. This alignment of all sectors increases the city's collective strength and determines a common direction. Community alignment to the will of God is a good spiritual principle, but it also makes economic sense. An STMC understands and serves a greater purpose than what is contained within its four walls. Find the redemptive purpose, see the needs, equip the leaders, develop a plan, and mobilize your city. As you do, you can make your small town mega church the equipping centre to serve your city in the direction it desires to go. It will become an epicentre for social change. As you gain credibility leading your city, you will enjoy a mega church presence and your church will continue to grow as a by-product. All of this can and will happen, but you have to believe in yourself, develop the skills God has given you, and create a church that facilitates community success.

Another STMC mindset is to be the *head, and not the tail*. We believe we have a responsibility before God to meet the needs as well as lead the community. In order to truly change a city or nation, we have to work from the top down. I saw this principle in my years in the mining industry. Safety or environmental policies and initiatives only had success when the management of the company made and enforced them as a core value. If we are to lead our cities, we have to engage the leaders. An STMC needs to create relational environments with people who have the ability to address needs and have access to sufficient resources to make lasting change. People of wealth and power are always looking for anyone who has answers to the problems of their cities. An STMC mindset understands that the problems of our city are not "their" problems; they are ours, too! As an STMC, we are not waiting for them to come up with answers. We are seeking the Lord to bring the solutions to them. We don't wait for someone to rise up so we can follow. We are proactive, creative, and determined to make a difference. We don't let the fact that we don't have the money to solve the problem stop us from facing it. We are only grasshoppers in the land of giants if we see ourselves that way. We may not have everything, but we can use to the fullness all that the Lord puts into our hands.

King David killed Goliath with a sling shot. We will never lead our cities into the promises of God if all we can see when we look forward are the giants that may resist our success. We hear the fear of the giants in the words of many church leaders… "We can't afford to do anything. We don't have the manpower to deal with problems outside of our church. We don't know how to deal with this stuff. It's not our calling. We don't get involved in city issues."

An STMC leader has a mindset that says, "We are well able to take this land!" It all starts in the mind. Do you believe you can become a mega church? If you say yes, then discipline your thoughts and words to agree with your intentions. Start to think and talk like a mega church and you are on your way to becoming one.

Another key mindset is in *how you see the local church in the community.* Many see the local church as only a small part of a city's dynamic. We have allowed the institutions of our nation to take over the social, moral, economic, and education programs of society. We do this because we think they are better able to deal with problems than we are, or that they have all the resources. This thinking has reduced the local church to serving only those we can entice within our four walls, or those with greater needs than we have. A key mindset of an STMC is to see the local church as the greatest strength of any city. We have to see ourselves as an entity that is the best answer to all of the problems the world is facing. I don't believe that this is pride or wishful thinking. The local church is the answer to mankind. It's not pride; it's just truth. I believe there is nothing greater than the local church. So why don't people come? People should flow into the local church the same way they flow to investment or self-help seminars. So why don't they? What should we do to reach them? An STMC has a mindset to create a church that people want to attend. They are facing real life problems. A series of messages about the meaning of Hebrew words, or debates about end times theology, don't address or even seem relevant to the real challenges people are facing today; these messages won't keep them coming back. Inviting people to special events like Easter and Christmas services really doesn't usually build the church either. These events may get people through the doors, but what they see and experience once they arrive will determine whether they will come again or not.

Small churches have mindsets and ways that repel people rather than draw them in. We put on a musical event with a low quality sound system that squeals and hisses. We put on a talent show that only shows we don't have any. We are inviting people to become like us or to be identified with us, but we lack professionalism, manners, creativity, and we speak a language that the world can't even understand… and we do things in a way that doesn't make any sense. The issues we raise and the way we raise them tend to just showcase how self-centered and out of touch we really are. People of success put a lot of time and effort into shaping their mindset. They have trained themselves to avoid negative, small-minded, defeated people, so they don't like most of our small church mindsets. They can see why we are small and have little hope of becoming anything of significance. Some try to address the issue with us, but many pastors and leaders feel threatened and reject their input. So the end result is that people stay away.

Many times during our services or special events, we are so busy being spiritual or visiting with our long-time Christian friends that a guest stands alone on the sidelines. An STMC does church in a different way. We work on the atmosphere of church. We do research to apply theology to the real world. We structure for success and we use professional principles. We work hard at creating a contemporary atmosphere. Restaurants have learned the value of fostering a contemporary atmosphere, and so should the church. We use flat screen monitors throughout the facility. We have music playing in the entranceway. People are encouraged to visit with everyone, and we all watch for an opportunity to welcome a new face. Visitors are very important and how we treat them will determine our visitor retention ratio.

Stepping into a church is like landing on Mars for some people. I remember the first time I attended one. I was twenty-eight years old. My parents had managed bars and motels for twenty-five years. Bars and clubs were familiar to me. When I went to church, it was so foreign. The people seemed weird. The music was okay, but different. The quietness made me feel self-conscious, especially when everyone stood or took communion. I was full of fear that someone would ask me about God or the Bible and I would have no answer for them—or even worse, that they would point me out in the crowd as a visitor. I didn't even know the Sunday School stories. I knew Jesus' name, but I don't think they would have liked the way I used it.

It was a long and hard transition. If it wasn't for a few who took the time to build a relationship with me and help me get used to the new world, I don't know if I would have made it. I don't think church should be so hard to join, so we have worked hard at fostering a welcoming environment of light-hearted joy.

Society today is used to top quality products and technology. If they come to church and see us using bad sound equipment, musicians who can't play, singers who can't sing, and a facility that is not maintained, they notice. A small church tends to accept low standards. Some even make it seem holy to be in lack or shortage. I hear it in many pastors' words. "We can't afford it… It's not about 'things'…" Well, yes, it is about some things. If we desire to reach a high-tech age, we can't connect with people using outdated equipment. If we want to lead people somewhere, it should be obvious very quickly that we have good leaders. If our God is a God that blesses His people, it should look like we are blessed! I don't drive a car that makes me look poor. I don't dress in cheap clothes to look humble and I don't wait for others to give me a handout so I can go out to a nice restaurant… and I certainly do not live in a tent! My life is not extravagant, but it is a life of excellence.

Our mindset is that *excellence is not an option!* We define excellence as "doing the very best you can with what you have in your hand." We go the extra mile in every service and in every way. Our goal is to create a five-star experience at every function we put our name to. We believe that every service matters! The best service we are doing is the one we are preparing for that day. We don't celebrate what we did last week; we anticipate what God will do through us *this* week. We look forward to every service, because every service matters. The environment we create could make the difference between someone meeting with God and getting saved or walking out of a poorly run service. The atmosphere makes a difference. If you went to a doctor's office and it was rundown, poorly staffed, unfriendly, and the doctor looked like he was the janitor, you would probably experience a miracle healing on the spot and get out of there as fast as you could! The quality and care of the atmosphere a person sees is a reflection of the quality and care of what they can't see.

We have to create an environment of excellence, and it doesn't just happen by itself. Excellence is really an attitude of appreciation. It shows the level of respect and stewardship of what the Lord has placed in our care. It's an outward expression of an inward quality. It doesn't have to cost a lot of money to be clean, friendly, and professional. We put "people-friendly" ushers at the doors so that the first experience everyone has when they arrive at church is to be met with a welcoming friendly face. We then put a colourful bulletin in their hands with pictures of our staff and their role in the church. We also give new people a tour of the facility, especially families with children who visit for the first time. We introduce them to the Kids Church team and show how we have taken precautions to keep their children safe while they learn, grow, and build relationships. Our facility hasn't always been the best one in town, but we have always strived for excellence.

We have just upgraded our facility in Drayton Valley. Our intention is to inspire three "wow" responses from those who attend for the first time. We have built a new entrance onto our facility that has eleven-foot ceilings. When you enter the main doors, it opens into a large room with high ceilings and it inspires an immediate "wow" reaction the first time you see it. We also upgraded our sanctuary and have built a new stage with lights and an impressive design. This also catches the attention of a first-time visitor. Then the music starts, and wow! What nice sound! We put a lot of our budget into creating good sound. It took years to train and develop our worship teams, but it has been worth every effort and every dollar spent. We also put effort into the quality and beauty of the facility, especially in areas like the women's bathrooms. We combine the "wow" factors of the facility with great sound in a lively and friendly atmosphere. We train teams to engage people in a friendly and joyful way. By the time the preacher hits the platform, our visitors usually already have three of four positive influences, and they are therefore open to hear what we have to say. We do this with every service, because every service matters.

We also have a mindset of excellence in all other functions of the church. We put extra effort into every detail. Anything that goes out to the community is done with excellence. The value of promoting excellence hit me one day while I was playing a game of golf. I had a weak moment and my ball went into the trees. As I searched for my ball, I found one that had a Nike checkmark on it. As soon as I saw the checkmark, I grabbed it with excitement, thinking, *This will be a good ball!* As I later thought about my reaction, I learned one of the greatest lessons about marketing. I have never used a Nike product in my life. I'm not into sports and pay very little attention to the top products they promote. I'm sure they have a good product, but that's not my point. I wondered why I thought they had a good product when I had never used them before. I realized that the opinion I had of their product was the opinion they had trained me to have! This demonstrates their great success in marketing their identity. If I was going to buy a pair of high-quality running shoes, I probably would have picked Nike shoes.

I realized that marketing was more than the advertisement of a function or event. Marketing was the process of teaching the community what we wanted them to think about us. We do this so that at the point of decision to change their lives, they would see the church as a credible option. This image is created one service at a time, one brochure at a time, one ad at a time, one event in the community at a time, or one visit to our facility at a time. I have been told by church growth experts that if you can get someone to enter your church for any reason, it increases the possibility of them getting saved or joining the church by eighty percent. This will only happen if they have a good experience when they arrive.

For the last seven years, we had one function for this specific purpose: we invited our community to a top quality production we call "Blast from the Past." We put on a three to four hour live production with singing and entertainment. We do it with skill and professionalism. This isn't for the church. It is intended to engage those who would never set foot into a church. Out of the new relationship, we invite them to other functions and services. Many have been led to the Lord and joined the church through the process. It all starts by creating a friendly environment of excellence that connects with where they are in their lives. Out of their positive first-time church experience, we hope they start to develop an attitude that church is a good place to be.

We should always be sensitive to those who didn't grow up in the church. The question we need to ask ourselves is this: "What do people say about their first visit?" Are they talking about five-star service or an experience they never want to have again? If we can get them talking positive about their experience, it encourages others to give it a chance as well. Word of mouth is the best and most cost-effective advertising you can get. Those who have been a part of the church for years may talk about a service or event, but they tend to only know other Christian people. New people are still totally connected to other pre-believers, so their account of the event reaches new unchurched ears. But in order for a good report to spread through the community, everything has to be done with excellence, and excellence doesn't just happen. We have to have a mindset of excellence, then follow through with intentional actions. The key attitude in an STMC is that *excellence is not optional!*

In the early days, we had very little resources, but we did the best we could with what we had in our hands. We put our sermons on tape with a portable cassette recorder. We created colourful covers for each series and put them in nice cases. We have continued to add to our multimedia presentations to this day. We now have the services and training courses on CD and DVD. We have a resource centre for our books and CDs. We stock the shelves with relevant materials that align with the teaching and vision of our church. The point is, don't wait until you have thousands of dollars to put out some products. Start with what you have and add to it as you grow. Even though the products may not have the quality of a church that has thousands of dollars of recording and editing equipment, just having them available to your people adds to the sense of a mega church. Many pastors don't record their teaching because they don't feel anyone would buy the products anyway. If this is you, this is a mindset you need to overcome. Listen to some of your messages and ask yourself these questions:

- If this was the first time I heard this preacher, would I be impressed?
- Would I understand his message?
- Was it boring?
- Would I give it to a friend to listen to?
- Would I go to the church every Sunday to listen to him?

If you listen to yourself and feel that you wouldn't cross the street to listen to this message if it was someone else preaching, it may be a good time to develop some preaching and presentation skills! Get some help! Get some mentors. We train our preaching teams. It takes years to become confident on the platform in a way that allows them to connect with the congregation. It is a lot like acting. I hate watching a TV show that has poor acting. You can tell they are acting and it ruins the sense of reality when it fails to draw you into the story. Preaching has a lot of the same dynamics to it. We have to preach, but not get caught doing it. What I mean is that we have to develop our skills as professional preachers to the point where we can tell a story and present a teaching with such reality that people are drawn into a living message that applies to their lives. If our mindset is that our message won't have much impact, it won't. If we think nothing will change, we are right. We need to have a mindset that believes God has spoken to us and that we are on a mission to bring this message in a simple, interesting, and profound way to as many as God sends to hear.

This brings us to another self defeating mindset. I hear pastors saying, "Everyone the Lord wanted to hear that message was here!" No, they weren't! That mindset serves no purpose except to massage our egos so we don't have to face another possibility—that they didn't come because it was not worth coming to! God wanted the leaders to come to the banquet, and they wouldn't come. He invited others to come, and they made excuses. Finally He said, "Go into the highways and biways and compel them to come!" Not everybody that God wants to be there, gets there! We should take the lack of attendance as an opportunity to face the problem. Was it the wrong subject? Was the timing of the function wrong? Are our services too long? Are we caring for the kids? Is the preacher just boring to listen to? Are they understanding the message? Are we not friendly? We should take every opportunity to ask ourselves the "why" questions. When you "face the reality," you can "find the opportunity" to develop your ministry and grow your church. We should never be complacent about our growth. If we stop forcing ourselves to grow, we won't! If we avoid the reality, we will create a fantasy!

By applying these simple yet powerful efforts to the quality of our church, we find ourselves doing small church in a big way! We have created an atmosphere in a small town, complete with the service quality and dynamics that you would normally only find in a big city mega church. The surprising thing is that it doesn't take as much money as you might think. We started with what we could afford and we are aggressively adding what we can as we grow. Our Drayton Valley location has grown to the size of a small town mega church, so our recent challenge was in changing its leadership roles and responsibilities, as well as finding or developing creative and yet relational programming.

We are shifting from a small intimate group with big vision to a medium-sized church. A larger church becomes less personal, so we are focussing on intimate relational programming throughout the week, like study or special interest cell groups. We are making the transition from doing small church in a big way to doing big church in a small way.

FOUR

THE LEADER'S PERSPECTIVE

Everything in life is about leadership or the lack thereof. Think about it. Your health is about your ability to care for yourself and lead your physical body in a way that increases its strength and lengthens life. Your marriage is about each individual taking leadership. We have to take intentional actions to make change; it doesn't just happen. Intentional actions are about leadership. When your leadership abilities increase, the more intentional actions become and the greater the change. Wealth creation is about your leadership ability to develop and discipline yourself to stick to a financial plan. Every area of life is governed by your leadership skills or lack thereof. Church is no different. The success of your church, or any department in your church, is about your collective leadership ability. Collective leadership ability is determined by the leadership strength of each individual and the synergy of the team. Increased leadership ability increases corporate capacity. Leading an effective and efficient team to maximum capacity is what builds a small town mega church.

In the New Testament parable quoted earlier, we see a man who gave some leaders talents, or money.

*"And to one he gave five talents, to another two, and to another one, **to each according to his own ability;** and immediately he went on a journey"* (Matthew 25:15, NKJV, emphasis added).

The money was distributed according to each one's ability. This truth applies to wealth creation or to church growth. A small church is always faced with financial challenges. In many cases, it isn't just about buying new equipment or starting a new program. The financial challenge is directly related to survival. We fast and we pray for increase. We let the needs be known. We take extra offerings. But in the end, if we don't overcome the present challenge and move forward in the vision, people get tired and discouraged giving to meet the same old recurring need. There is always need. God's people are very willing and faithful to give to meet a new need, especially if the new need has been created from success or unmanageable circumstance. I want to be clear that I believe in calling out to God to meet our need, as He is our source and supply. But I also believe in increasing our abilities so that God can release more resources. We should face our financial challenges with a positive attitude that proclaims that our God is able to meet this need by causing gold dust to fall from thin air. The problem with God solving our problems supernaturally is that it doesn't increase our abilities. We haven't learned any new skill and we don't have any better understanding of how to solve our problem, manage change, grow a church, raise capital, or do business God's way. The inevitable end is that we will return right back to the place of our leadership capacity—an atmosphere of bondage and need.

We cannot do the same things over and over and expect different results. Old habits and old leadership ways will do exactly what it sounds like: they will lead you. The problem is that they will lead you back to the same old place. We need to change to make change! The leadership skills and methods that got you to this pressure point are the very things that will keep you at or returning to that same pressure point. Pressure is a sign that the maximum capacity of your team is near. The key to moving forward and breaking out of the pressure point is to increase your collective abilities. Financial pressure points are not really about money; they are about change. People in the congregation very quickly recognize any inability of leaders to develop the health and strength of the church or their lack of skill in managing greater resources. They start to limit their giving according to their perception of our ability. If we refuse to learn and grow as leaders, their perception becomes our reality. The whole church becomes limited by perceptions, not facts. *To increase resources, we have to increase ability!* The opposite remains true as well. If we continually increase our collective leadership and professional abilities, we move into unlimited corporate potential.

The more focus you put on training your leaders in the synergy of corporate team dynamics, the more resources will be released and the faster the church will grow. Trusting the Lord for a miracle at the last minute sounds spiritual. I hear celebrations all the time about the last minute provision of God. I celebrate with them. But the greatest supernatural last minute provision of God example in the Bible was during the wilderness experience. God had to supernaturally provide for His people when they were in disobedience and a wrong spirit. Manna and quail came to meet the need, but as soon as they crossed over into the promised land, the manna stopped. Why? Because now they had the resources to provide for themselves. Now they needed wisdom to manage the resources. How did they cross over? Joshua and Caleb had a different spirit. They said, "We are well able to take this land." God had gone before them, but they still had to take it according to their abilities.

We are in the same circumstance today. God has gone before us, but we still have to take the land or put effort into bringing in the harvest. The increase in your harvest will be a direct reflection of the increase of your collective ability.

I have had the privilege of meeting some of the largest mega church leaders in the world. They are all unique in their approach to ministry, but all have one thing in common: they are great leaders. They have developed their skills to build teams, cast vision, mobilize people, manage resources, and carry out strategic plans. A lack of any of these components will be the main limiting factor of the size and effectiveness of your church, not the devil.

In the gospel of Luke, Chapter 19, we see another leadership principle of increase: the servant who took the one mina and caused it to multiply to ten was given authority over ten cities. The one with five was given authority over five. The one who did nothing, or was a lazy steward, had what he held in his hand taken away and given to the one who possessed ten. Stewardship of the minas released authority over cities. The one who was the greatest steward of what was placed in his hand received the increase of his efforts plus the increase given to him that he didn't work for. I believe this is a biblical pattern. If we are good stewards of what the Lord has placed in our hands, we receive the fruit of our labours as well as the blessing of increase from God. Luke talks about the principle of stewardship in Chapter 16.

"He who is faithful in what is least is faithful also in much; and he who is unjust in what is least is unjust also in much. Therefore if you have not been faithful in the unrighteous mammon, who will commit to your trust the true riches? And if you have not been faithful in what is another man's, who will give you what is your own?" (Luke 16:10-12, NKJV)

God tests us with the natural before He trusts us with the supernatural. The way we handle the natural resources God releases to us has a lot to do with the spiritual favour and strength of our church. Influence can come to some by personality or charisma, but true influence and direction-setting authority comes from the level of our stewardship. As we combine these two principles, we can see a formula that looks like this: *Increased ability equals increased resources, and the quality of the stewardship determines the level of authority.*

A leader of a small town mega church is a leader who understands and daily pursues God while at the same time strategically improving the collective strength of his church's corporate capacity. This is done by adding to the church's combined abilities and improving its systematic efficiency.

Many leaders refuse to pursue success out of a fear of people. Many see leadership ambition in the church as pride or lack of trust in God. They see church growth and success being all up to God.

They think an attitude of poverty and lack is somehow holy and right. They think a pastor should get rewarded in heaven but suffer for Jesus on the earth, that a church should just do the best it can with what the Lord has given it and nothing more. Thankfully, there are many others who see money as good and not evil, that abundance for every good work is a Biblical promise, that highly motivated and successful people can also be humble, pure, and Kingdom-motivated. STMC leaders will see wealth as a tool for fullness. They understand that it can't be done without resources, that someone needs to be paying the bills! They believe that if the pastors and leaders are blessed, everyone is blessed. They understand and embrace the wisdom and strength of marketplace leaders. They see being in business as an honourable ministry blessed by God. They are leaders who have the ability to see that God intends for us to have an abundance for every good work, and they will cheer you on in your success. These same people will challenge you when you think small, feel small, or limit God's work in your life and ministry.

Poverty-minded people will keep you in the pressure of poverty and need. If you ignore their voices and teach and believe for success, your success will be criticized. If you accommodate their views, those able and willing to build with you will see the inevitable failure ahead and stop supporting your efforts. There is pressure either way, so the question is this: which pressure would you prefer? You get to choose! The pressure of lack or the pressure of the criticism you will get from poverty-minded people because of your success. I have chosen the pressure of success.

We have many choices to make in the leadership of a church. Tensions between the natural and spiritual responsibilities are numerous. Do we give the extra revenue we generate to the poor? Or do we pay down the mortgage? Or do we add to our staff? Or do we improve our facility? Are we here to facilitate the family of God, or to reach the lost? Is the main focus inward or outward? Is the journey to the purpose of God about my development, or about Him working through me to others? Do I need to fix me first, and if I do, when am I good enough to actually do what I am called to do? Is money good? Should we teach that God will prosper His children, or should we stay humble and poor? What perspective of theology is closest to the truth? Who do I listen to? Are we about law, or grace? Is success about raising up superstar sons and daughters, or is it about an equal opportunity body ministry? Do we compromise quality for inclusion? Why is the church even here?

Of course, we can see that the full answer to the majority of these questions is… yes. We are here for both the individual and the body, God's people and the lost. We are also here to be humble and to prosper! It may sound oversimplified to ponder these questions, but your perceptions of these issues are the building blocks that form your reality. Each of the issues you could list (and you should) have a subtle influence on your perspective of church and the role of ministry. They are subtle and seemingly insignificant when they stand alone, but when combined they create your reality. Your perception of the role of money will determine how you raise and handle the resources God releases to your care. The size of your church and influence you achieve are also defined by your perceptions. It becomes like faith as it sets the boundaries of your capacity and ability to succeed. Your perception becomes your reality.

This can work in your favour as well. If you work at changing your perspective, you can shape your reality. The process of change is about making many subtle choices. This process defines your values, relationships, theology, emphasis, and success. What does success look like to you? Who is in your life after you succeed? Who and what won't be in your life?

A few years ago, I had a friend of mine, Dr. Jim Garvin, the founder and current CEO of Obed Corporation, help us to develop our business owners group, and he asked the group a very good question: If God gave you twenty-five million dollars to work with, what would you do next? I liked that thought. If God solved your financial problems, do you have a plan? If God answered your prayers and a hundred people joined the church this week, could you handle the integration of new families, teach the new converts, and still be efficiently managing the church? This thinking is the essence of a small town mega church. We are constantly defining our beliefs, furthering the vision, and preparing for the rapid growth of the church. Our main goal is to live in the fullness of God in every way. We are pursuing the gifts and the fruit of the Spirit, the humility, and the prosperity of God, the lost, and the found. We are not choosing one or the other. We want it all. As author Dr. Ed Delph, founder of Nation Strategy, likes to say, "It is not *either/or*; it is *and*."

If you aspire to become a small town mega church, you need to be passionately and aggressively pursuing your full potential. Status quo mediocrity is not enough. We intentionally press ourselves to the edge of our collective capacity. When you press yourself to the edge of your potential, the pressure is on, things happen fast, and mistakes are made. Mistakes are part of the learning process. Trying to avoid all mistakes will limit your progress. Crises and mistakes will define you. How you react in a crises or when you make a mistake will define your identity and determine your credibility. Troubles will define your values. It forces clarity of vision and purpose and it shapes the character of your team. Nobody seeks trouble, but we realize that how we react to trouble will shape who we are, and this response can become a part of our internal DNA. The blessings of God make it all worthwhile, but how we respond to the troubles we face in the journey defines our sense of worth and will determine our true core values.

The choices made on this journey of discovery are many and will never end. As we mature, our understanding increases and deepens, so we adjust the guiding values accordingly. The goal of a small town mega church leadership team is to be as consistent as possible. The guiding values should be applied to newcomers as well as the seasoned members of the congregation. Many times, we treat newcomers with grace but put great pressure on those who have been around for a while. We should treat the people the same way we treat our staff. Our families should live within the same guiding rules and liberties as we extend to the church. Many leaders can be very hard on their kids as they expect them to live up to some high standard they never met themselves.

I was saved by grace and the grace of God alone sustains me. One of the main core values of our church is to extend grace to all. It's only by the undeserved favour of God that I am saved, and certainly the ministry He has blessed me with goes way beyond what I could ever deserve. Grace is grace! Thank you, Jesus!

The goal of church leadership is to establish the guidelines and define your values with enough clarity to be used by all and not hide the fact that there is still a consequence of sin. Grace does not mean that there are no consequences. What it does mean, to us at least, is that although there are consequences to failure, it doesn't change our core value of relationship. When Adam and Eve were cast out from the garden, God went with them. He has maintained relationship throughout our failures. Grace recognizes consequence, but refuses abandonment. How we respond to failure as an organization reveals our true inner core values. Seasons of failure of a staff or family member will reveal how we apply the value of equality. Do we treat them with the same guiding values as others? When we experience the failure of a team member, we are forced to remove them from ministry until they can be restored. Grace doesn't remove consequence. This has not been a problem, because people understand the philosophy behind the guideline and will normally remove themselves. As leaders, our job is to be consistent. If we remove a leader one time and ignore the failure of another the next because they are our best worship leader or preacher, we by actions establish a two-tier corrective action system. This very quickly becomes an "us and them" environment. Inconsistency in this area of leadership will undermine your leadership, weaken the team, and allow all kinds of doorways for devils to work against the church from the inside. We need to settle in our hearts that all people are important, not just the ones that agree with us. The guidelines are there for a reason, and if they are blessed by God, they are for us all.

The best way to teach our core values is by example. Failure of leadership team members are opportunities to display real life examples of our core values. Every eye is on the problem. Everyone is watching and talking about what has happened. The leadership of a small town mega church needs to communicate clearly and yet discretely. We must stay true to our core values and extend grace by refusing to abandon people in their failure, while at the same time displaying obvious consequences for their actions. These consistent character qualities are the strength of a leader and will determine the success level of your church. Inner guiding core values are the raw materials of leadership strength. Troubles are the hammer and chisel in the hand of God to shape these inner values until we have a true outward expression of an inward grace.

A small town mega church leader has to be willing and passionate about growing faster than his or her church. You are one of the most important assets to your vision. You cannot be smaller than your next level of success. The growth rate, size, and quality of your church is largely determined by your personal growth and leadership ability. You cannot stay small and expect a big church. This thought brings out another principle. You are important, but your goal must be to be replaceable. We are there to work ourselves out of a job.

An important role at any level of mega church leadership is to be the carriers of the vision. I tell our team that any conversation anywhere, with any age, needs somehow to be about the vision. In real estate, it's about location, location, location. In church, it's vision, vision, vision. Building a small town mega church has a lot to do with the leadership's ability to turn a prophetic vision into an apostolic or tangible working reality. This is why I am big on structures and systems. Many believe that structures and systems limit the freedom of God, but I am on the opposite side of the thought. I believe structures, systems, and efficient, well-managed strategies are what liberates a church while maintaining a common direction and goal. Without structure, no one can find their role or place.

Defined structures and system norms allow decision-making to be done without a lot of red tape. Systems for evangelism, discipleship, mentoring, corrective actions, leadership development, or any other dimension of the vision, are liberating if done with the right spirit and used in a right way. I taught a great deal on this issue in *The Power to Effect Change*, in the chapters on corporate team dynamics. Leadership structure is the strength and protection of a local church. Structures and systems are not the enemy. The use of the structures and systems will determine their value.

Structures can be used to limit and control if used by someone who has that motivation. Our goal while leading a small town mega church is to be consistent in our vision, values, and ways while allowing freedom of expression.

As we have become a multi-site church, this has become an interesting thing to watch. Each of our locations have the same vision, structures, values, systems, and leadership style, but the outward expressions are very diverse. Our original intention was to franchise the multi-site church with every detail remaining exactly the same as the other locations. This is a great goal, but it does limit some unique, site specific expression. In a larger picture, we looked at what our church sites in foreign nations would look like. If they are franchised to look exactly like the Canadian church, we would limit the freedom of cultural expression. This can happen within a city. Each church site must embody in some sense the social, ethnical, and economical diversity of its region. The goal is not to achieve an exact expression, but instead to share consistent vision, structures, systems, values, and leadership dynamics. Our church services have some diverse expressions, but they still feel the same. I think this is good. In business, there is a saying, "He who sweeps the floor gets to choose the broom." This applies here as well. He who does the work of the ministry chooses the flow of the ministry.

We have a clear vision and some guiding values that are followed by all, but we also do our best to embrace diversity and encourage creative thinking as normal elements of change.

FIVE

VISION NEEDS VALUES

I need to first be clear that we consider prayer, the word, integrity, missions, evangelism, and worship as core values that are common to all churches, including ours. My intention in this context is to show some of the other core values that guide us in our daily activities. Knowing your core values is important, as they are the inner guidelines that regulate our reactions, our self-esteem, and our sense of success. Our inner core values are being shaped day by day, individually and corporately, whether we are aware of the process or not. Our values get established by our relationship interactions, our experiences, and our perspective on those experiences. We cannot avoid core values; we all have them. We can, however, be intentional towards creating them and consciously work to clarify and reinforce the positive and weed out the negative. The more stable and consistent our core values, the more stable our lives and ministry. An inner core value of truth will not allow you to lie without conviction. A core value of success will immediately expose small thinking or defeated emotions.

CORE VALUE #1: VISION

The Bible teaches that without vision, the people will perish (see Proverbs 29:18). When we cannot see a vision for our lives, we start to lose hope for the future. Anyone or any church that has lost their vision will also lose its passion. We start to reduce ourselves to the status quo. We start to limit our thinking to our present circumstances, or get focussed on some negative experiences of the past instead of the possibilities for the future. We need to understand that we are not limited by the size of our city. We are not limited by the present size of our church. We are not even limited by the devil. We are only limited by the size of our vision! Churches that don't grow usually don't lack talent; they lack strategic vision!

We need to write a plain vision for our personal lives, then for our church and every department in it. Write it down, read it out loud to yourself, and talk about it every chance you get. The voice with the greatest influence on your future is your own! In *The Power to Effect Change*, I point out that very few pastors can describe a vision for their church outside of doing weddings, funerals, and ministering to whoever shows up on Sunday mornings. This shows me that we can get so focussed on doing the work that's right in front of us that we lose sight of, or never get around to defining, a greater vision.

A new church is faced with many challenges and pressures.

The pressure to survive a church plant will tempt us to embrace everyone and every ministry or idea that comes through the door. We can become so aware of, or sensitive to, the opinions of people that we start to adjust what we normally would say or do so that the people will stay. We feel the need to show we are listening to them and desire to accommodate their interests. We adjust the volume of the music, we sing the songs they suggest, and we even preach what they want to hear. The process may be done with good intentions, but in the end when we fail to live up to their expectations or we finally decide to do what the Lord told us to do in the first place, those who no longer get their way leave. But now they have developed relationships and have some influence in your church, so they very seldom leave alone!

As we plant churches, I have learned that a clear and consistent vision with wise strategies will allow people to make the choice very quickly whether they belong with us or not. When they want us to embrace their vision or reshape our identity in order for them to join, we have to make a choice. Are we here to gather a crowd, or are we here to carry out a vision? Never compromise what the Lord told you to be and to do just to keep people in the church. If the issue is the level of quality, professionalism, friendliness, or lack of clarity, or they desire to understand your theology, you should respond with professional courtesy and answer all their questions and improve your performance as much as you possibly can. But when the issue is the vision, the direction, the flow of service, the focus you have on the seventeen to twenty-five age group or the music they enjoy, you shouldn't start changing everything in hopes that someone might stay.

When people want to leave our church, we have to have

enough confidence in God to let them go! God the Father is constantly pruning the tree. If we resist the pruning process, we may hold on to those who are really not with us in spirit, and eventually there will be a breaking point of relationship and they will split the church. We will never compromise the vision just to please some people. Everyone has their ideas, past experiences, and gifting. We embrace all people and integrate them into the church as much as we can, but they must find their place within the vision; we will not abandon the vision to give them place.

When we are a small church, we want all people to come so that we can quickly become a strong, stable church. We envision the great prayer warriors who will come, along with the rich, the influential, the worship leaders and musicians, and we fantasize on how glorious it will be. The reality is that in the beginning we are like King David and attract the indebted, discouraged, and discontented. Many come with their own idea of church. They have their own vision or they have their way of doing things from their old church. Many have had a time in their lives when God was doing something awesome. They know what caused the revival experience to break out and are sure that if they did the same things again, they would have another life-changing experience. Those who are prophetic think they can prophecy themselves out of anything, those who have a missions heart believe giving to missions is the answer, and those who are evangelistic believe they should have healing and deliverance services every Sunday. Worshippers want to ignore everybody else and just press into God for their life-changing experience. The fact is, they are all right. God shows up in all of these things. But we can't be all these things all the time. So we have to know who we are in the Lord and what He has called us to do.

The best way to build a strong church is to be true to who you are. At our church, we have many locations, and each one is unique. The structures, strategies, programming, big picture of city transformation, and leadership styles are all very similar, but the expressions are diverse. We build the church to reflect the personality and natural strength of the people who lead it, and we create an atmosphere that connects with our local target group and redemptive purpose for the city. Drayton Valley is a vision-driven, entrepreneurial, creative, leadership-oriented community. There are many self-made millionaires. The church is a reflection of the community dynamic. Over half of our adult population in that location is directly involved in the business world. Messages, seminars, or meetings about strategic leadership inspire the people of our Drayton Valley location. The city of Fort Saskatchewan is a blue collar community that serves heavy industry. The predominant gifting and ministry flow there is prophetic intercession worship. The experience of God in the service is a higher priority in this location than the strategic flow. The service atmosphere is centered on the worship experience and prophetic giftings. In the one location, the emphasis is on His purpose; in the other its emphasis is experiencing His presence. We have a common Life Church logo, the same team structures and program content, but very diverse service flows and atmosphere.

We have developed taglines for our locations to reflect the nature of those specific sites. In Drayton Valley, the tagline is "Living life on Purpose!" This reflects the strategic, purpose-driven entrepreneurial nature of that city. In Fort Saskatchewan, the tagline reads, "Living in His Presence!" This reflects the life of a worshipper. Another of our locations uses "Finding Life in Jesus!" as the tagline to reflect its redemptive purpose.

Every church needs to be able answer some simple, yet defining questions.

1. Who are we? (There is an inherent strength God has placed within your fellowship. When you define the strength, you can build programming to embrace your uniqueness rather than copying the status quo of others.)

2. Who are we called to reach? (A church that can't define its customer doesn't have a customer.)

3. Do our messages connect with our target group?

4. Are we using language they understand?

5. Are we relevant to their lives?

6. Does what we say about ourselves connect to the desired target group?

7. What comes natural to us?

8. What atmosphere should we create?

9. What is our core message? (Jesus is always the core of all we do and all we are, but each church has a core message that represents its part of the body of Christ and reflects the gifting God has given it.)

It's very important to be able to answer these kinds of questions. They define who you are and will guide the direction you go. They also align your church to a common identity and purpose. A church that doesn't know who it is will ultimately try to please everyone. When a church falls into this trap, it can be seen in its flow of service. They have something for the young, something for the traditional, something for the newcomer, and something for the seasoned. The problem is that by trying to create a church that pleases everyone, they end up not really pleasing anyone and fights start over music, service flow, or expressions. It's like a radio station that plays opera, then a rock song, then a country song, then jazz, then bluegrass, all in an attempt to have something for everyone. In an attempt to please everyone, they please no one.

You need to know who you are and be bold enough to just be good at being you. There will be many who will come and try to gain influence and position by attempting to get you to do things their way. If you surrender to the pressure to change just to keep the numbers up in the church, you will never define your identity or build a church that knows who and what it is. We have to have the confidence in our vision to not compromise what the Lord has told us to do and to be who He has created us to be, even if some will not stay in the church. When people want to leave the church, we have to have the strength to let them go. When you stay true to your vision and define your identity, you will eventually create strength with a one voice, one sound unity. When this happens, it becomes self-weeding. People who come can clearly see who we are and what we are doing, and by seeing these things, they can easily decide whether or not they belong. Those who connect with our vision become sons and daughters of the house. They quickly take ownership of the vision and find their place. There is no way to win by compromising. We can only win if we don't play the game. A church that doesn't know who it is finds it hard to say no to anything. It is pressured by many good works and there are always some in the group who have another passion or perspective on church purpose.

When we know who we are and what the Lord has called us to do, we can separate these issues into categories of opportunity or destiny. We ask ourselves continually, is this just a good opportunity or is this something we should pursue because it is part of our destiny? There are many good works going on in every part of the world. We need to be good at being who the Lord created us to be. We can stay busy and do good things and still miss the fullness of the purpose of God for our lives and our church. Who are you and what have you been created to do? I call this our redemptive purpose or the reason we were created and gifted the way we are. Find it and stay true to it and let it be the anchor point of everything else you do.

A church tends to grow from visionary and ambitious leaders. They are full of passion and purpose and have a determination to succeed. Out of their success, the people come. They come with needs and ideas. Meeting the need causes us to start shifting our focus to management and maintenance. We start to add management and maintenance people to our staff and teams. This is needed, but there is a danger in creating an overemphasized management and maintenance oriented leadership team. A church can experience rapid growth when pastors have lots of time to spend with newcomers. They are the ones who tend to be the most passionate and can motivate others to join. When pastors or visionaries get so busy looking after the people who are already a part of the church, they spend much less time reaching out to or meeting newcomers. This slows church growth. Many have tried to motivate the congregation to bring their friends, evangelize their area of the city, and have pursued other evangelistic strategies. The problem is most people don't find reaching out that easy to do. For many, it is the very reason they joined a church in the first place; they wanted an environment to find and build friendships.

I have heard the frustrations of pastors over the years as they tried to grow their churches by mobilizing their people to reach out. I believe we all should reach out, and some really do, but the vast majority of people are more comfortable with people who come to us rather than us going to them. We have decided to focus our existing church members on the preparation to receive, help, and maintain the new people. When the new people are well cared for, the visionary, passionate pastors and leaders are freed to meet more new people and further the vision. We can then use our events and social programming as an atmosphere of engagement for the visionary builders. I will cover more on the subject of maintenance programming in later sections.

Core Value #2: Grace

I have already given some examples of our application of grace, so I won't go over it again, but I do want to emphasise some key points.

When Moses faced the Red Sea, he proclaimed, "Behold the salvation of our God." It showed that he understood the willingness of our God to help us in our times of trouble. He doesn't help us because we deserve it, but rather because we know we don't, but have put our trust in Him. I face life and ministry with this faith in God. When the odds are against me and life is not cooperating with me, I do what Moses did. I stand up before the congregation and proclaim, "Behold... or watch what the Lord will do to get us through!" Not because we deserve it, but because He loves us and we are on a journey of His design. God brought us here, and God will get us through!

The Bible says that it's the goodness of God that leads us to change (see Romans 2:24), not our programs, rules, or legalistic opinions. True change comes when you experience the reality of the love of God in your life and you want to let others experience it through you. Legalism tries to achieve purity, but ultimately binds rather than liberates, controls rather than releases, condemns rather than convicts, and becomes works oriented rather than grace oriented. We are here to preach and represent the good news! The good news is that no matter how bad you think you are, the grace of God is still there for you. God is good even when we aren't! No matter how pure we think we are, we still need to depend on His grace. Grace is not an excuse for sin. The grace of God extended to me gives me the motivation to live an abundant life in the fullness of God. He will never stop extending grace, no matter what we do, but intentional sin will limit our ability to receive it.

I want to state again that *grace recognizes consequence, but refuses abandonment.*

CORE VALUE #3—RELATIONSHIP

The Bible, and the Christian faith in general, is all about relationship. The strength of a local church or a church network can also be judged by the strength of their relationships. We tend to put a lot of time and effort into tangible things like sound equipment or resource materials. We work on teaching depth, leadership skill, and the development of the individual or corporate strengths, but neglect the most important thing: relationship. How many small churches put leadership or team relationship building activities into their annual budget? How many senior staff will take the junior staff on an all-expense retreat just for the sake of building relationship strength? How many boards would approve such a thing in the budget in the first place? We haven't arrived at all-expense retreats yet, but we do cover the costs of many relationship-based daily activities. We do lunch meetings a lot. They are very good environments to build relationship and influence one another towards change. We used to order pizza or Chinese food, but lately we have been doing salads and fruit. This is due to an increased fitness awareness amongst our team. We still do lattes for all sessions, though, and have created a coffee shop fellowship atmosphere in the entrance of our churches to facilitate relationship. We are putting in specialty coffee machines, pop and fruit dispensers, music, and flat screen TVs complete with leather couches and coffee tables. Why? Because *relationship is a core value.* So we create quality environments to facilitate it. We don't just do ministry together; we do life together.

Our staff and my best friends are the same people. Staff members are hired from two dimensions. The first dimension is that they are friends who have displayed potential, and the second is that they are people who have proven great potential and have become friends. In our world, skill is not enough. Relationship is the glue of all we do and the sustaining strength of every success we enjoy.

Our teams are not just task-oriented. We have a phrase to reflect our core value of relationship: we remind ourselves continually that it is "people over task." When we analyze our progress, we ask ourselves some tough questions. Have we put the task at a higher importance than the people who carry out the task? Has the task become more important than those it was meant to serve? If the answer is yes, then we have violated one or more of our core values and need to make adjustments. A leadership team without definable core values has no way of knowing when they are off-track and are becoming something they never intended to be. When our core values are clear, they work like red flags, getting our attention and steering us back onto the path we set out to follow. Many fallen individuals and organizations can look back and see with certainty that if they had stayed true to their original core values, they wouldn't have gotten into such trouble.

Relationship tensions on a team are a sign of change. Sometimes it is simply a sign that the maximum potential has been reached and that some realignments and redefinition of the roles of each member is needed. Organizational growth defines roles, relationships, and responsibilities. A Sunday School teacher that is doing a great job with thirty children may not be trained or even willing to lead the department when we are working with one hundred and fifty kids. Now the issues are about scheduling teachers, developing curriculum, and attending staff meetings. There are totally new skill sets involved and the person leading that department has to choose to grow or let go. Those who are training that leader need to make them aware of these impending changes long before that department actually arrives at the shift in leadership dynamic.

Every department is faced with the same shift. Even the founding mom and pop pastors are forced to grow or let go. We have chosen to grow, but even with our greatest growth efforts, we need to consciously discipline ourselves to let go of many daily responsibilities. This can and needs to be done and it is done through efficient systems and strong relationships. I let go because we have other leaders I trust and work with who I believe are even better at the tasks than I am. The trust I have in them is from proven skill, good character, and strong relationship with myself and other team members.

When adding to our staff, we use the two dimensions of relationship and skill, even if there are members of our own families that want the job. It almost goes without saying that all pastors want to have their family involved in the vision. But how? We already have the relationship if it's a family member or long-term friend, but it is only a good idea to bring them onto the team if they have the matching skills.

One of the most interesting issues we had to overcome when our children joined our staff was that they had to learn that we were now their bosses, not just mom or dad. There are protocols they need to follow even though they are family members or long-term friends. Being a family member of one of our existing team leaders will get you to the front line of opportunity in itself. We let it be known that family of our staff can choose anything they wish to be a part of, and we will give them a shot at it. The deal is not without conditions. If they are not able to carry the responsibility or develop the skills to show that they can do the job as well or better than anyone else, or that we are at least getting good value for our investment, they will be removed. I hope we see our great-grandchildren working successfully for the church! When relationship is a core value, we should do all we can to work with our families and friends and to make those who join us from the outside very quickly feel like both.

CORE VALUE #4: EQUALITY

This one shouldn't have to be in our core value list, but it is. If we are not intentional about equality between the ages, sexes, social status, or ethnic groups, we will fall into the historic pattern of society's social and structural elitism. This may be subtle in a church, but if you are looking for the expressions of inequality, you will find it there in some form. I don't want to challenge anyone's theology, but inequality is seen in many forms and I will only list a few.

Staff meetings that have very little presence of women or youth are an expression of inequality. Boards and leadership teams with the absence of the same are displaying a form of social elitism.

Churches that will not recognize women in ministry could argue the issue of biblical authority, but they should not limit or belittle their contribution. We believe in husband and wife leadership teams. To the best of our ability, we hire or work with both the husband and wife. They are both licensed and ordained by Life Church International. The moral issues we face in the ministry today are so complex, and can get into our lives with such subtle progressive influence, that we don't see them developing until it's too late. We need our wives at our side. It is one of the greatest protections we can have against moral failure. The team approach also helps to keep the family and marriage strong and on common ground. The couples spend their time together planning the future of their ministry and their marriage.

Most churches would not be enjoying the successes they have were it not for women in ministry. They are doing the work, whether they get the credit or not. We decided right from day one to recognize their leadership and give them a direction-setting voice in the church. We could be criticized for our perspective of theology in the area of women in church authority, but our experience shows an obvious hand of God in the women leaders of our organization and I would trust them with my life.

The decision-making process in general can display inequality. We have established a consensus-style leadership environment. I am ultimately responsible for all decisions, but I certainly don't have the complete perspective or experience to deal with every area without input from others.

The consensus-style agreement we have with our team looks like this. I want to hear the passionate opinion of all our leaders on any subject that applies to their department or touches their heart. I will give them all an equal opportunity to express their perspective as passionately as they desire. All input will be considered, but as I am the one who carries the greatest responsibility if things go wrong, they must allow me the privilege, or authority, to make the final decision. The vast majority of the time, we can make a decision by consensus and an obvious solution presents itself. When we are not clear or we cannot come to a consensus, I will make a decision and I ask for all to come on board until a better idea or avenue becomes available. Once a decision is made by consensus, or by what may be called executive decision, we function as one voice. We will not use words like, "This is what he or she wants." We use words that express collective agreement, like "This is what we want," or "This is what we decided." There is never a time when we all get everything we want or things go exactly the way we would like them to go. The goal is not total agreement of the team, but rather a sense that everyone has been heard and feels that their opinions matter and that their input is contributing to and shaping the nature of the organization.

CORE VALUE #5: SYNERGY

Synergy is created when the production or achievement of the thing produced is greater than the sum of all its parts. Good leadership is about the ability to increase corporate capacity through team synergy. I think creating synergy on a team is one of the greatest joys of a leader. There are so many possibilities when you define what unique giftings, interests, experience, goals, age, or even cultural background can bring to a team.

Corporate synergy does not mean that everyone is lining up to a preset image and conformed totally to one style of ministry. It is about creating an environment of diversity that releases everyone to their fullest potential while accomplishing a common goal. A small church can multiply its potential by producing synergy. Every member of a church has a gifting, skill, or experience that can add something to the success of the team. Everyone can carry some responsibility. While our church was still around fifty people, we started to define departments and position team leaders to accomplish specific tasks. I will cover this subject in greater detail, but my point for now is that the sooner you start creating the teams, the faster your church will grow.

The main key to corporate synergy is to know where you are trying to go. Once the destination is defined, you can decide on the vehicle you need in order to complete the journey. Corporate synergy in a church is such a powerful principle that many churches that have been in existence for a long season of time can actually determine their redemptive purpose or the thing they were created to do by observing the combined strength of their members. They can look back in their history and clearly see definable traits and ministry successes. This gives them the focus for their vision. I believe the Lord sends us the people we need to carry out the redemptive purpose, but we get so busy maintaining the programs and facilities or caring for the people that we don't stop or take the time to make an assessment of our strength. When we do an asset assessment and find the majority of our church is gifted in missions, we can be fairly confident that the Lord wants us in missions. In our Drayton Valley location, where over half of the adult population of our church is directly involved in business, it becomes obvious that the Lord wants us to focus on leadership development and corporate team dynamics.

It's very important for a leader to know the gifting and leadership perspective of their team. Vision driven leaders do not need a lot of other visionaries around them. They need some strong maintenance-oriented leaders on their team. On the other hand, a maintenance-oriented leader should embrace the visionaries. Visionaries without maintenance-oriented people will build and move forward so fast that they can destroy the very people they are trying to help. They can get so focussed on the task or the vision that they become totally blinded to the warning signs of stress and danger on the team. People that fly water bomber aircraft can get so fixed on putting out the fire that they ignore the danger signs, lose track of elevation, and fly the plane right into the ground. They call this "target fixation." A church leader can have the same problem. We can get so focussed on the vision, so determined to win the battle, that we lose the ability to maintain stability. The result is that, if we're not careful, we can fly the church right into the ground.

Maintenance-oriented leaders can have the opposite problem. They can be so intense about caring for the equipment, the facility, the programs, or the people—or are caught in a constant state of preparation—that they never show up for the fire. Synergy is the combined fullness of both.

Synergy is also about age group. We are not trying to bridge the generation gap; we are out to remove it. There is no need for a generation gap. We need to embrace the generations and allow them to add their strength to the team. The question I would ask you is this: Does your youth have a say in your church? Are they properly represented on your leadership team? Do they get to preach and teach? Do they have a voice in the atmosphere and flow of the service? Are all the ages properly represented, gifts identified and embraced, and are they all given equal opportunity and equal voice? If you can say yes, then you are well on your way to a corporate, generational synergy.

Do an asset assessment of your people of all ages and determine what you are naturally good at, what stirs your passion, and what touches the heart of your church. This can be measured by the giving in a church. When you touch the heart of the people, they will financially support the cause. The heart and the wallet seem to open at the same time.

With all of the diversity in human nature, character traits and gifting, creating synergy can be overwhelming to some. The goal is to embrace diversity, develop individual character, and partner their strength with the strengths of other team members. If we work at completing one another rather than competing with each other, creating synergy can be motivating in itself. Relationship and communication are the keys to experiencing synergy within diversity. See diversity as an opportunity for expansion, not a threat to status quo.

CORE VALUE #6: RESTORATION

The corrective action policy, along with our restoration procedures, are two other areas that need to be carried out with consistency. If there is any place for the golden rule to be applied, it would be in these two areas. When we are faced with implementing corrective action, we should not ask, *What should we do?* But rather, *What would we want others to do to me, if I were the one who had failed?* The motivation needs to be correction, not punishment; restoration, not rejection. Are we really worried about the individual, or are we just trying to defend our position or our name? A lot of reaction to failure seems to be done in attempt to protect the leaders, the name, or the image of the organization. What about the restoration of the one who failed? Are we really trying to defend the integrity of the Christian faith, or are we just trying to separate ourselves from the problem?

An organization that does not have a restoration procedure is an organization that will point out the dirt but not want or be prepared to deal with it. If we are not willing to deal with the dirt, we shouldn't dig it up. It takes the predetermined collective strategic will of any leadership team to walk with someone who has failed, and to stay with it for as long as it takes to achieve restoration. There are always consequences to failure that may remove someone from pulpit ministry. Likewise, someone who has a problem with child molestation should not be repositioned back into the children's ministry of the church. This would be like asking an alcoholic to manage a liquor store. Someone who has been charged with theft probably shouldn't be the one handling the money from the offering. We have to use wisdom, but I do believe in restoration. The restored person may not function in the same role they did in the past, but they can still find and experience the fullness of God, be restored, and be used by the Lord in other ways.

The line of restoration is a hard line to draw. How far will we go to restore an individual, and to what level of ministry? We have seen people who have prison records for all kinds of criminal activities, including murder, find their way behind pulpits to give their testimony or be the star attraction at an evangelistic function. But God help the pastor that had a marriage failure who, in spite of all the best intentions, couldn't be restored! Traditional systems of restoration make it easier for us to forgive killing each other than to forgive someone who has gone through a divorce. I am all for defending marriage, and we fight for it with all we are. My point is this: Sometimes, even when the best efforts are made, we still can't rescue a marriage. What now? Are these people eliminated from their calling for good? Can they function at any level of recognized ministry? I know what we have decided as an organization, and my goal is not to impose our guidelines on you. Rather, my goal is to encourage you to think through this kind of situation in advance and come up with a policy that you feel you can use with consistency.

These policies are not guided by theology; they are guided by our application of theology. We have to feel we could stand before God and give an account for our actions. An overuse of correction can cause as much damage to God's kingdom as not enough. It's a very difficult line to draw, but it must be drawn. Once the policy is determined, it is very important to be consistent in every situation. The circumstances vary, but our policy and procedures can be consistent. Ask yourselves, what level of ministry will we restore them to? Can a woman be released to ministry if her husband has fallen away, or is she also finished? How long should the minimum restoration time be? How should we hold them accountable, and who should do it? Who should know about the failure? Is it a public issue? How does it affect their relationship with you? Does it affect other team members in a negative way? Where do we stand on divorce and remarriage?

I try to do all we can within our church leadership team to restore an individual, but when we are dealing with circumstances that are beyond our level of experience or expertise, I have no problem sending them to other trained professionals in the community. We have many family and support services that are run by the government. These leaders do not have to teach my people theology, but they can give some very good practical advice and steps in regards to overcoming trials. A counsellor doesn't have to be born again to help us, but they most definitely need to be pro-church. I arrange and build these relationships in advance so that when a family violence or crisis situation presents itself, I already have in mind social workers, psychologists, or other professionals I trust. I honour their training and they do all they can to teach from a pro-faith perspective. A small church very seldom has the professionals in the congregation itself, so trusted professional relationships in the community can be a great asset.

When we are working on restoration, we do all we can to determine whether there is true repentance or they are just sorry they got caught! When we see a genuine Godly sorrow, we move towards restoration. Regret without Godly sorrow will eventually repeat itself in some form, so we just wait it out.

A common question we face is, *When do I confront people if they are negative about our church and are having a negative influence on other people?* I don't confront them right away if I don't have to. I watch for the level of relationship support they have in the church. Someone that has strong relationships out of charisma or compassion can take a lot of people with them if they leave. I watch and wait for that individual to start to get on other people's nerves. They will! When I hear my leaders, team members, or some of the core strength of the church start to say things like, "Why doesn't someone do something about this?" I know the influence that individual may have enjoyed is weak or gone. At that time, I can step into the situation and be as aggressive as I need to be to force change or exodus and still retain the people that were once supporting their cause. If you deal with the problem while the individual has compassionate or relational support, you will turn a large group of your congregation against you—and your problem will be bigger than ever. Be patient. There is a time to be aggressive, but timing is everything. If the right timing is used, you can deal with a negative situation and increase the respect of your congregation at the same time. In future circumstances, people will remember how you handled the last one and give you lots of time and support to deal with current situations.

Troubles are always an opportunity to learn and grow. They are also a chance to demonstrate wisdom in leadership. We always need to leave the door open for restoration. This means we have to deal with situations all the while keeping our hearts right in the process, so that in the event that the individual wants to reconnect with the church, or has repented of their ways, we have an open door to give them another chance. This is grace.

Grace doesn't mean that there are no guidelines or consequences. A person being restored needs to be in cooperation and agreement with the process. A reluctance to follow through with restoration will lead right back into another dead end situation. Don't let it take your time. All we have to offer are the tools and opportunities for restoration; after that, the ball is in their court. If they put in the effort, we work with them, but when we get more concerned about their well-being than they are, we are done. We leave the door open to them for another attempt in the future, but we reduce the staff member's involvement until we see an effort on their part.

I once had a circumstance where a woman said that her husband never spent any time with her. During counsel, I asked him what kind of ice cream she liked. After twenty plus years of marriage, he didn't know. So my challenge was for him to take enough time off to take his wife on a date and have an ice cream with her. All he had to do was be able to tell me in our next session what kind of ice cream his wife enjoyed, and after that we would progress to another step to resolve their problem. He never did. So I concluded that if he was not going to put enough effort or take the time to take his wife for an ice cream cone, he wouldn't want to do what needed to be done to fix their marriage. I was done. About two years later, their marriage failed and he was done, too. You cannot force change. You can only give people the tools and opportunity to change.

Restoration has the same nature to it. We can only provide the opportunity by having a guiding policy and willing leaders. The effort needs to come from the one being restored. If they don't put any effort into their restoration, neither do we. It may be sad that they are wasting their lives, but it is even sadder when they can waste the time and energy of a whole leadership team in the process. Develop a self-directed systematic approach, a step by step process of restoration for all to follow, that doesn't require a lot of your time or input to keep it moving forward.

Core Value #7—Honour

The Bible instructs us to honour those who rule over us in the Lord. This is a hard concept in itself for some. Someone rules over us? Wow! We are equal in value, but we have different levels of responsibility.

Why do we use titles? If the church is all about relationship why not just be on a first name basis and leave it at that? Some even argue that we don't say plumber Frank or carpenter John, so why say Pastor Gary? There isn't any authoritative intent in using titles. We do it for two reasons. The first is that we have a relationship-based church where friendships are formed between team members. I don't want them to get to a place where they know they have a friend but don't have a pastor. When things are going wrong and they need some advice or correction, it is easier to receive from someone you see as your pastor, and not just your friend. The second reason is that the title of pastor doesn't have any legal purpose, but it does have a great relational one. Every time someone calls me Pastor, it is an expression of love, respect, and the value I have in their life. Being called Pastor is like being called dad. I would feel funny calling my dad by his first name. Even if I could, I wouldn't. I want to call him dad. It is an expression of affection. I hope all who call me pastor do so out of love from their heart, not in submission to a title. When I hear the title, it always reminds me of the role I have in their lives. It challenges me to another level of leadership and encourages me to live at a higher level of character and professionalism. If I let myself think and talk like I was just a friend, it would rob us both of a greater blessing. I also believe in honouring the office. We may have some issues with the Queen of England and the independence of Canada, or have different political views than our Prime Minister, but when we are in their presence, we should honour the office they represent. Using the title of pastor is another opportunity to give honour to those who are giving all they can to serve the people of God. It also provides us an opportunity to express the humility that is working in our own lives. I believe that as we give the gift of honour, we will reap what we sow and honour will be released back to us.

Core value #8—Protocols

Protocols are very important as the church grows. As you establish department heads and leaders, you have to discipline yourself to honour their positions by using proper protocols.

During my years of mining, I saw the violation of staff protocol happen almost on a daily basis. In the leadership structure of a mine, there is a manager, followed by a superintendant, then department general managers, shift bosses, lead hands, and crews—just to name a few. A mine manager has the authority to go out on the worksite and give instruction to anyone he chooses, but if he does it without following protocols, he weakens the strength of his management team. To bypass a department head and go directly to the team sends a signal that the department head is not important, that the team doesn't have to listen to them, that they can talk directly to the manager. If the manager has an issue with the's crew performance and talks directly to them instead of talking to them through the proper channels (superintendent, department manager, and shift boss), he has just weakened the leadership credibility of the team and has demonstrated a lack of trust with the department heads or shift boss.

It works the same in a church. If we have enough confidence to establish someone as a youth pastor, or any other department leader, we should respect their leadership responsibility enough to go to them first. If things need to be changed, allow them to initiate the change in their own style and personality. As long as the issue gets addressed, it is of no value to undermine their leadership or bypass their input. A good leader at any level will want to have a chance to discuss the issue before it is brought to their team rather than being blindsided in public, or worse yet, get informed by the team that changes are being made.

CORE VALUE #9—RESPONSIBLE LEADERSHIP

A well-trained leader will become a responsible leader. During my years in the mining industry, there were countless times when I heard crew members say things like, "I saw that problem a few weeks ago," or "I knew about that problem!" When asked why they didn't report or do something about it, they would say, "Well, it's not my problem." This is a very frustrating answer for any supervisor. I often thought about how this mentality gets developed. I am all for defined roles and responsibilities in the workplace, even in a church. But when our defined role becomes our excuse for not addressing an obvious problem or doing something we know needs to be done, we are heading for disaster. This gets even worse if we start thinking the task is below us or our job title. When we are looking for leaders, we obviously pay attention to their gifts and strengths, but we pay even closer attention to their response to need and their willingness to pitch in beyond their job description. We watch for those who jump in to stack chairs or sweep a floor. Those who will only volunteer when the pulpit is open will not make great leaders. Responsible leaders will take ownership of the vision, the program quality, people care, facility maintenance, as well as the cleanliness and overall well-being of the church. Leadership is not about a title; it's about having an ability to see a need, the willingness to take initiative, and the strength to carry responsibility.

A leader who will not take responsible action when a natural need presents itself will be a leader who will be selective in spiritual ministry as well. We have three main guidelines when considering a team leader.

1. Are they in agreement with the vision?
2. Are they in right relationship with other leaders?
3. Do they financially support the church?

An individual who doesn't take personal ownership of the vision, walks independently from other leaders, or refuses to carry some financial responsibility will eventually build a ministry with the same dynamics. Luke 16 teaches that God will not trust us with true riches if we can't be trusted with the natural things He puts in our hands. Watching how a potential leader deals with the natural resources God places in his care will reveal how they will carry spiritual leadership. Individuals who will notice and pick up a gum wrapper, clean the walkway, or stack chairs without being asked will also notice spiritual needs and take responsible actions. They are the ones who will be there at your side when the pressure is on. They will do all they can to help. They volunteer for service and are creative problem solvers. Identifying a potential leader can be brought down to this one principle: When there is trouble, who takes ownership of the problem and starts moving forward towards a positive solution? They are your leaders!

Core Value #10—Work

This is a four-letter word that many church people seem to avoid. The ratio between the attendance and the workers is usually: Eighty percent attendees to twenty percent workers. Sometimes this is due to structures in place that do not allow for more leaders. It can also be due to existing leaders not being willing to give opportunities to others. But sometimes it is simply an attitude. I see many church members and leaders who have an attitude that the Lord will build the church. They quote the scripture that says that unless the Lord builds the house, we labour in vain. I have had many pastors tell me that they believe all they need to do is pray and the Lord will do the rest. I wish it was that way. I believe we need to pray, but I also believe we are the hands and feet and visible manifestation of the body of Christ. He is the head, but we are the hands and feet.

I recently spent about two years doing research. I travelled to many mega church organizations around the world and found some common factors.

1. They were great leaders.
2. They built great teams.
3. They built and managed systems very well.
4. Most of all, *they work very hard.*

Building a small town mega church will take a lot of work! A leader of a small town mega church cannot treat their role as a job or a career complete with a forty-hour week with evenings and weekends off. It will take over your life. The STMC leader cannot fit the church around his life; he has to come to a place where building the church *is* his life.

Almost everything I do has something to do with building our church. This may sound crazy to some, but those who have built a mega church will say amen. Work is one of the main core values of our team. It has become such a core value that our greatest problem is making sure our staff actually takes time off. Instead of work being a discipline and time-off being a passion, work has become a passion and time-off has become a discipline. We hold each other accountable to stop working.

We have applied a Biblical principle. During the creation account, God worked for six days and rested on the seventh. We have all tried to apply that same pattern to our lives, but the reality is that we are not God. He worked till He was done, and then He rested. We are never done. We work until we are so tired that we need to take a break. The problem is that my doctor told me that it takes three days for our bodies to go into rest, and we have to stay resting for another seven to actually feel refreshed. He told me that taking two extra days to rest after a conference wasn't helping me much. God gave me an insight into the creation account. God worked until He was done, and then He rested. Man's first day was a day of rest, so that he could go to work. We are to enter into the rest of the Lord. We have applied this principle by using our day-timers and corporate calendars to schedule rest breaks before we work. Before we have a conference, or before a season of busyness, we try to build in some time of rest to prepare ourselves for work. It has worked much better for those of us who tend to be workaholics.

I believe in work. I understand that the Hebrew word for work and the word for worship is the same one. God put us into the garden to worship through work! Even though work is one of the pillars of our core values, it still has its limitations. A small town mega church leader cannot sustain the pace by simply working harder. Our time and energy max out very quickly. By hard work alone, we will only build a church measured in the one to two hundred range. We need to work hard and we need to work smart. Once we have the core value of hard work functioning in our lives, we need to spend our time increasing our knowledge, developing our skills, and improving our program efficiency and team synergy to work smarter not harder. There are growth barriers that are reached that cannot be overcome by working harder; we must work smarter. Teamwork is not optional for a small town mega church. Without teamwork, you cannot grow past a church that is really just a home group with a worship team. Later, I will talk more about the teams of the local church.

In past chapters, I have covered a lot about our core value of excellence, so I will just recap on a few items here.

We believe in doing all things with excellence. How we define excellence is what determines our attitude or emphasis. I like to define excellence as "doing the best you can with what you have." It's understandable that a small church budget can't buy the biggest and best of everything, or have the facilities and programming of a church of five thousand. This shouldn't deter us, though, from doing the best we can with what we have. The cleanliness of a facility can be maximized without a large budget. The low cost of technology allows for bulletins of excellence. We moved from power point projectors in our sanctuaries to flat screen TVs. They are not only clearer, but also less expensive. Any media used in the church should be well done. The programs are now affordable and many of the young people know how to run them. This means that excellent multimedia is within the reach of a small church. When we do a service, we are very conscious of our level of excellence. The seminars we put on have always been done well. We decorate our tables and create a unique atmosphere for each one. When we put on an event for the community, it is done with excellence. This has built us a reputation for putting value into everything we do.

The worship team may be small, but they should strive to do the best they possibly can. Many people are willing to play, but are not willing to practice. I wouldn't go so far as to agree with the old adage that practice makes perfect, but I would say that practice is the first stop on the road to excellence.

Anything that has our logo on it or is connected to our church in any way is done with excellence.

SIX

LIBERATING STRUCTURES THAT ACTIVATE AND EMPOWER

Structures are valuable if you design them to liberate rather than contain, release rather than control. Most of the time, the structure isn't the problem; the problem is usually found in how the structure is being used. It is a natural process to develop a centralized governing body. The problem is that it usually becomes a rigid or static structure that eventually limits or contains. This static structure reduces or eliminates the ability to rearrange your team to accommodate what the Lord is doing at any given time. We tend to build structures and programs in the hope that people will lead them and the Lord will fill them. This will work for a season of time if you have identified what the Lord is doing in that season. The problem is that the Lord moves on to other areas of ministry with a different emphasis, possibly a different flow, or He starts to work through a different age group. If our structures are static, we will try to contain or force the new to fit into the old wineskin... and we all know what happens next. We end up spending more time defending our structures and putting out relationship conflicts than we do growing the church.

A fluid leadership structure isn't without tensions either, as there are many changes on any journey. A fluid leadership structure has the same principle as a flock of ducks as they fly. One takes the lead for a season while the others follow in the air stream to preserve energy and increase speed and longevity. As the journey continues, the lead duck pulls back and another takes the lead position for a season of time. This principle applies to all levels of leadership, including me. I may be the organizational head, but in practice I too must get out of the way and let others take the lead. Now, I may not go back to Sunday School teaching or worship leading, but I do go on to other activities to further the success of the church. If I refuse to let go of my present identity and tasks, I become the focal point of strength and momentum. This may boost my ego, but it will ultimately slow or stop the growth and strength of the church—or at least its collective potential. A fluid leadership team is connected to the big picture and sees their role as having an equal opportunity to serve, whether they are leading a team or serving one. The goal for each team member is to be the kind of team member we want to have working for us when we are the leader. Our staff should be equippers of the saints, who do the work of the ministry so even their role changes during the various seasons of church growth. As soon as we start to see ministry as a hierarchy, where position and title becomes the goal rather than serving a greater cause, we start to have a rigid or static leadership structure. If this is the problem, removing structure won't address the issue. The real issue is the motivation of the leaders within the structure. Denominational structure is not the limiting factor of church growth. The structures are good, so what happens? If we take our eyes off of our church and look to the corporate world of business, we can see the answer. The process of moving from a mom and pop small business to a corporate team dynamic is a big step. Many don't make it due to an inability to move away from "hands-on" leadership to a "governance role" and style. The larger the organization becomes, the more pressure is put on the intimate relationships that were developed at the mom and pop stage. The larger the corporation, the more communication, reporting, and guiding the system needs.

In the same pattern as the visionary church I spoke of earlier, a new corporation has passion, determination, and the will of a pioneer to succeed. With ambition and focus, the business flourishes. The success, however, creates a demand for maintenance. The visionary pioneers see maintenance systems as a burden, so they start to bring management oriented leaders onto the team. The problem is that success soon brings aboard more maintenance managers than visionaries and the focus shifts from risking it all with passion and enthusiasm to quality controls and system maintenance.

This overemphasis of management is the number one reason corporate growth slows to predictable numbers on a growth chart. We need to keep the passion and enthusiasm of a pioneer in corporate management. We need vision *and* maintenance. An overemphasis on either one will limit and even war against long-term success. An overemphasis on maintenance will allow controlling people to rise to the top of the leadership structure. These kinds of people will bring with them a collective will to enforce, protect, and maintain status quo. This is done to maintain the integrity of an organization, but the outcome is the killing of the corporate spirit and the limitation of passionate pioneer zeal.

On the other side of the issue, passion and zeal without maintenance structures and systems cannot be sustained. Without guidelines, people will do what they think to be right in their own eyes, and chaos and conflict will soon follow. The zeal will cause the visionary team to chase after the quick fix or the fast track to success. They tend to jump on the bandwagon of the next thing that comes along. Lots of projects get started, but few survive long-term. A lack of consistent vision and strategy will breed confusion, distrust, and allow strong personality and charismatic people the platform from which to promote the next great thing that will solve problems and lead to quick successes.

All areas of ministry need to be guided by consistent values, systems, procedures, and philosophies. In almost every situation, there are many eyes watching for the response of our leaders. No one is expecting flawless leadership, but they do and should expect us to be consistent. We need to be guided by core values and procedures that are embraced and applied with consistency over a long period of time. When values and procedures are applied one day, but not the next, mistrust and insecurity are bred in a congregation towards the leadership team, and low confidence will be bred in the ability of the leaders themselves. The more consistent our values, corrective action policies, funding practice, delegated ministry, promotion practices, and even our personal leadership dynamics, the more trust, security, and confidence will result in the church.

A good system put in place with wrong motivations will be used to control or manipulate rather than release and bless. A poor system with right motives may be well-intentioned, but still be limited in impact. We need both. Good systems and right motives! The central strength of a liberating structure is found in core values. It's core values that determine the reaction to problems or opportunities, and they are the motivation behind the use of all structures and systems.

LIBERATING STRUCTURES: THE TEAMS

We have a slogan we use in our church to reflect our strategic purpose: "Train a leader to build a team, to accomplish a task!" The goal is to build self-motivated, self-correcting leadership teams. I covered this in *The Power to Effect Change*, but I would like to give an overview of it here as well.

Any team can learn to be self-motivated and self-correcting if we give them the chance. We have to determine our goal before we start. If our goal is contained in the task itself, we will not delegate the responsibility to anyone we know has not had proven leadership ability. In a church, we get so focussed on the task or the quality of an event that we get paranoid about any possible mistakes of the team. This fear of failure forces us into a "hands-on" leadership approach to any function. We may have successful events with this leadership dynamic, but we will never build self-motivated, self-correcting teams. The goal of leadership is to set the vision, determine the reality of the present situation, build a team to accomplish the task, and work with them to develop a time-based strategy. A leader needs to stay in a governance role if he or she wishes to build a strong self-motivated team.

Team leaders need to identify possible team members, but must also get them approved before asking them to actually become team members. This is due, in Canada at least, to the Freedom of Information Act. There are things a senior pastor may know about an individual that cannot be passed on without their written consent. To accommodate this law, we have a principle in which the senior pastor's final approval of all team members is required (this applies to all departments). I allow each team to choose who they want to work with, so my answer is a simple yes or no answer. If the answer is no, don't ask why, because the information is protected by law and cannot be released without written permission.

Once the vision is set and the reality is defined, we must let the team determine the route. If we have the right people in the right places, they will have the gifting to move the project forward. They may not get from Point A to Point B as fast as you would, but as long as they are making progress you need to keep out of their way. The time-based goals are important to the success of the team. The team will move forward based on their sometimes limited experience. We need to let them go the way they wish to go for a season of time. When we reach the pre-determined time-based checkpoint, we can analyze their success. We should ask questions like, "If we continue on in this direction, will we reach our predetermined goal?" If the answer is no, the next question a team will ask you as a leader is, "What should we do?" It's very important at this stage of the journey not to answer the question but rather to send the same question back to the team. As the team thinks it through and makes the necessary adjustments, they have just learned the skill of self-correcting. Human nature has a pendulum effect to it and they will usually overcorrect and get off-track in the opposite direction. Again, a manager must wait for the team to reach another predetermined checkpoint and analyze the progress again. Using the same approach, you can guide without directing a team to success. As they work through the process of analyzing and making adjustments to their progress, they are becoming self-correcting and self-motivated.

A corporate manager that won't risk the possible failure of a team will step in and lead. We do this with good motives. We want the team or the event to be a success. The reality is that we can have a successful event, but still not train a team. When this becomes a normal occurrence, you will find an atmosphere of willing workers who will serve and follow instruction, but as soon as the leader isn't there to give direction or sort out a problem, the team progress slows or goes into total chaos. We are not here to gather followers; we are here to create leaders. When we accomplish a task using the other approach, the task can actually be less than perfect, but in the long run you have still built strength into the church by creating self-motivated and self-correcting teams. Any team that learns how to be self-motivated and self-correcting on the first task attempt will have a much greater success rate on the next attempt. By using this process of team development, we can create self-correcting and self-motivated teams in three tasks. Any team that develops the skills will be a productive team for as long as they are in the church. It is worth the risk!

SEVEN

THE TRAINING LADDER: PASTORS IN TRAINING PROGRAM

R andy Rye and his wife Joan are the site pastors of the Drayton Valley location and vice president of international ministries. Randy and I both have a mining background. When we started to train those who expressed interest in becoming pastors, I had this idea to call them our "PIT crew." The acronym stands for Pastors In Training.

The real challenge to any church organization is to find people who are willing *and* able. There are many who are willing, but lack the determination, character, emotional strength, or the skills needed to actually survive clergy ministry. I didn't want to be the one to judge their potential or their resolve. I didn't want to say yes to the ones I thought would succeed and no to the others. Mistakes can be made that way. There are those who can impress you for a season, but eventually fall apart when the real pressure is on. This is very disappointing, because it takes about four years to train a good leader. As a result, you have a lot of time invested in them.

I also wanted to remove the personality issue. Many times leaders are chosen simply because we like them, not because they are the best at what they do or will actually stay focussed for the long haul. In the Bible, many were called by God when others couldn't see the potential He had placed in them. No one thought David would become the leader of the nation—but he did! Many times in a church, we don't listen to the Davids that God has placed in our lives. They are the ones who are faithful, but don't stand out in the crowd. They seem to have very little influence and have gifts that seem too small to make much of a difference. God sees the heart and many times He chooses to speak through the Davids in our midst. If we set our eyes on the charismatic, the popular, or the extreme gifted ones and shut out the voice of the humble servants, we can miss the voice of God. He will put a life-changing message or destiny-establishing direction into a humble, small, and seemingly insignificant package. This is a test of our hearts. A prideful heart will not listen to anything perceived to be beneath it.

We wanted to have a system that was self-weeding, a system that allowed everyone to take a shot at their dreams—a way that anyone could succeed and a way we could monitor the progress of all who felt called. Our PIT crew is processed through about eighteen departments. Each pastor in training must get a working knowledge of all eighteen departments before we would consider them for a site pastor position. They spend time working with all the departments learning the skills, philosophies, and programming of each. Each pastor in training must get signed off in that department by the department head. Anyone who is not motivated enough to learn how to run all eighteen of them will not survive a career as a site pastor. On the other hand, anyone who is motivated, develops the skills, and gets approval of the leaders is a good candidate for becoming a site pastor. This allows for potential to surface that we may not have seen in the beginning, as well as causing those who just wanted a title to step aside. We have lay leaders going through the pastors in training program just to be more effective in the local church. Many of them have no plans in the near future of leaving to run their own work, but they have become vital members of the local team. Now they are like the five virgins in the Bible who were prepared when the bridegroom showed up and the door opened. They may never step into full-time clergy ministry, but they will always have that option available to them and they have developed skills that make them a valued and flexible member of any team. I call the process "performance oriented promotion." I am not very impressed by all the talk I hear in the body about what people say they *could* do. Show me! We will know them by their fruit!

The training ladder has some other guiding values like, "Short-term people serve long-term people." I realized that we were heading into some roller coaster rides of highs and lows if we used very gifted but short-term people. We tend to set charismatic or gifted people in leadership even when we know they don't intend or probably won't stay with us for a long period of time. When we establish them as department leaders, the team follows their lead and things usually grow and prosper. The problem is that most of the time these highly gifted leaders are good at leading people, but not good at training. This gets the job done for a season, but as soon as they move on, the team falters and fails and we start over again.

The number one commitment I am watching for in a potential leader is a long-term intention. We all know that there are things that arise that force us to change our careers or locations, and at times there is very little that can be done. The intention, however, can be heard in their conversations right upfront. We watch and listen for good quality people who talk like their intention is to be with us for a long time. These people aren't always the most charismatic, or even the most gifted, but every skill they do master returns fruit to the local church for years to come. The energy, skill, or charisma of a short-term individual can be added to the team to enhance its performance, but should never become the anchor or the driving force. They are there to lift the long-term team members to a new level and strength.

You should continually ask yourself, "How big a hole will be left in that department if this person left?" If the hole is huge, we need to fill it in advance. Our goal is to be three layers deep in all department tasks. We should have the one doing the task, one other that is almost as experienced as they are, and yet another who has developed enough of the skills to fill in when needed. We use this approach in all areas of ministry, from drummers to pastoral staffing! We have an intentional atmosphere that promotes the strength and success of the team and reduces the superstar syndrome to a minimum. Everyone is important, but no one should be irreplaceable, even me! The strength of a leader can be measured by his or her capacity to leave. If your church slows or stops moving forward when you leave, it's not always the fault of the team; it is usually an issue of leadership dynamics.

The training ladder concept puts the responsibility of personal and ministry development on the individual and allows them to progress at the rate they choose to go. It also allows them to stop at any stage of the training for as long as they wish. This removes the pressure from senior leaders and gives them a clear focus group to work with. The training ladder system is so simple to track that any individual can see clearly how far they have come and how much more is yet to be achieved! Many churches want their people to reach maturity, then start doing ministry, but the Biblical pattern is actually the other way around. People were called to ministry, then rose to maturity! People mature by doing the work of the ministry, not watching.

There are eighteen key departments on the pastors in training ladder.

EIGHT

PREPARING YOUR TEAMS

1. THE LIFE CONNECTION TEAM

The LCT is responsible for the integration and well-being of new people. They also stay connected to the people who attend, but are not engaged in a department or relationship group of the church.

The ushers work with the Life Connection Team to collect visitor cards during the services. This gives the LCT the information and permission to follow up on the visitor with a phone call. The initial phone call should be done within a couple of days of the visit. The LCT then watches for that person or family to return. Upon their return, the team works at integration. They start to spend time with the new family, determining their faith background or simply answering questions about the church. They find out about their family dynamic (for instance, is it a single parent household, a family with small children, a family with teens, and so on) and connect them to the proper department leaders. They ask about their interests and hobbies (such as cooking, fishing, hunting, camping, horseback riding, weight lifting, etc.). This helps to direct them to small groups of similar interest. They ask questions about past church experience and involvement and if there's anything they would be interested in getting involved in at our church. What giftings do they have? When we can answer these questions, we can be more effective in helping families find friends, purpose, and connection to the local church.

The LCT continues the follow-up until the individual is connected to a small relational group and has integrated into the church. Then they move on to other new people. They do not have to deal with troubles in the church, family counselling, or do the job of the helps ministry team. They are only helping the people connect to the church. Any need identified or trouble spotted needs only to be passed on to the pastoral care team, at which point their responsibility is completed.

2. THE DISCIPLESHIP CORE

There are three levels of Discipleship Core. Level three is all about relationships with the body. This is friendship and activity based. During their time together, they build friendships, answer questions about God or church, find out more about the interests or needs of the individual, and connect them to a department in the church that matches their gifting and interest.

At level two of the DC program, leaders are being developed.

This individual would have two or more DC team leaders under their care. They maintain and mentor those who are engaging the people.

At level one, the individual is now becoming a leader of a department or is carrying greater levels of responsibility. Their DC would consist of other department heads or other ministry leaders.

3. Intercessory Prayer Teams

There are six prayer teams in the church. Each one has a specific focus that address defined issues.

1. The Spiritual Warfare Team addresses national and regional historic spiritual strongholds through research and prophetic revelation.
2. The Family Prayer Team.
3. The open session Mountain Movers Prayer Team, which deals with community issues and makes declarations of God's blessing over the city's streets or schools.
4. The Marketplace Prayer Team, which prays specifically for the businesses of the church.
5. The prayer shields for our leaders, like Jesus prayed for Peter in Luke 22:32 (*"That our faith won't fail"*).
6. The open session prayer meetings to cry unto the Lord.

4. MARKETPLACE MINISTRIES

These are the gatekeepers of our city. We believe in marketplace ministry. What is allowed into our cities and how we develop for the future is in the hands of our marketplace leaders. They have the influence to open or close the gate to just about anything that presents itself in our city. They have the influence to lobby government, the skill to develop a blueprint of community transformation, and the ability to shoulder the vision of the local church. We need more than just their wealth; we need their wisdom and God-given influence!

5. CHURCH STAFF TEAM

A site pastor candidate must develop a skill in dealing with paid and volunteer staff.

6. ADMINISTRATION TEAM

The administration of the church budget, facility use, staffing requirements, service flow, and programming quality are all a part of the administration team's role.

7. MARKETING TEAM

Internal marketing of the vision, values, and present focus is very important to a fast-paced, ever-changing church environment. We need to keep all stakeholders informed. I have heard it taught that we need to restate the vision every twenty-eight days. This shows the need for internal marketing of the vision, program options, and staff changes that are taking place now or in the near future.

External marketing is about creating a community identity so that, at the point of decision, people will turn to your church.

8. Pastoral Care Team

This team is involved with the care of every age and every need. This is probably the most time-consuming function of our team. Those who get tired of people's problems or hate all the time that dealing with people will consume should reconsider a career as a clergy site pastor.

9. Kids Ministry Team

They are not just the church of tomorrow; they are a vital part of the church today. Kids Church is not about babysitting so that adults can have time to carry out the work of the real ministry. Rather, Kids Church is about the early stages of development of destiny. We are building the foundation of greatness into the next generation. Over the years, we have seen kids make career choices to be in clergy ministry and take specific action steps to prepare for their future.

10. Youth Ministry Team

This is also not just a department of the church, but a major emphasis. Everything we do includes input from our youth leaders. I had a pastor call me a few years ago about an ad he had just seen on TV. It said, "If your teenagers aren't trying to borrow your car, is it really worth driving?" I say it's the same for the church. If the youth are not trying to take over the church, is it really worth building? Our youth emphasis does not mean we do all things like a youth church would do, with loud music and activities. It means we invite them into the leadership and decision-making process of the church by embracing their creativity and energy. The atmosphere we create has the goal of being youth friendly, but not adult exclusive!

11. WORSHIP TEAM

Worship is more than music. Worship is about living in His presence and a life totally surrendered to His will. It is about a lifestyle reflected in a talent, an outward public expression on the platform reflecting an inward personal reality of God. Everyone can and should worship. Leaders need to engage and promote a contagious worship experience.

Our worship teams practice to develop their skill, but their greater goal is to inspire one another to press into God. Pressing into God is contagious and is triggered by those who are called to lead.

12. MISSIONS TEAM

It is important to know the face of your mission initiative. For us, it is training leaders, planting churches, and mobilizing the body of Christ to transform cities and nations. We believe in meeting the needs of the poor, but we intend to end systemic poverty by creating sustainable economies through leadership development and micro-business opportunities.

We have a four-part statement that describes what we see as

the mission of LCI. First, leadership training and development. Second, team building and corporate team dynamics. Third, the planting and growth of the local church. Fourth, effective community engagement through the principles of *The Power to Effect Change*.

13. Media Team

One picture is still worth a thousand words. Communication through multimedia is the greatest tool for churches in the recent history of Christianity. Church leaders do not have to become the most creative or technical person on the team, but they should keep informed enough to appreciate the potential of using media. We try to incorporate up-to-date technology and training so that those who are meeting the need for the local church are also developing a skill they can use in their careers.

14. Social Functions Team

This is one of the key areas of church strength and stability. Social functions are great evangelistic opportunities, but we use them to strengthen and build relationships on the teams as they accomplish tasks and engage the congregation at large.

15. Hospitality Team (Ushers, Greeters, Service flow)

They are the first faces a new person meets when they walk in the door. The opinion of a guest will form in the first few minutes he or she is in the facility. Personal interaction from the parking lot to the chosen seat adds to the five-star church experience.

16. Clean-up/Set-up/Tear-down Crews

One of the skills a pastor in training needs to develop is in building and managing crews to accomplish natural tasks. Many will volunteer to preach, but disappear when it's time to work. When a church is small and renting space, the set up crew is vital. As the church grows to having its own facility, there is janitorial work and facility maintenance projects that need willing and able crews to address. Finding, motivating, and showing appreciation to volunteers is one of the greatest gifts a pastor can have. Many stop serving because they don't feel they are appreciated.

17. Listening Prayer Team

This is a special ministry created to deal with the root issues of our past. It is confidential and powerful as the Lord reveals Himself in the context of an individual's trauma or crises from their past. We are not looking at the crises in themselves; we are looking for the presence and voice of the Lord during them. It is amazing to hear the testimonies of what the Lord said or revealed to an individual during these prayer sessions.

18. Board and Legal Team

In Canada, there are many items that fall under the Freedom of Information Act that make it hard for pastors and leaders to deal with some very serious issues. We are not allowed to share information about some criminal or violent activities of an individual without that person's written consent. There are also times when we are required by law to call social services and let them take the lead in an investigation. We are also required to keep our board members informed and follow established guidelines laid out in our church constitution and involve them while making amendments. All pastors in training need to clearly understand the legal guidelines and laws governing the church.

Leadership is key, and everyone is a leader. I am aware that everyone has a different level of ability and that the people skills vary with each individual, but I believe all have been brought into this world for a purpose. Every person can contribute something. Their gifts and perspective have been designed to meet a need. Our job as managers is to match the gift, people skill, and ability to a specific need. There are those who can lead ten, those who can lead a hundred, and there are leaders of thousands.

Long-term success is determined by the proper placement of each individual. Everyone can carry some responsibility. Some may only wish to cut the grass, and that's okay if that is the level of responsibility they can handle. Someone who has a greater leadership capacity, but wishes to cut the grass, is robbing two people: They rob themselves of the growth and experience of carrying more responsibility, and they also rob the one who may not be able to carry more responsibility but would have felt good about the contribution they were making by cutting the grass. Keeping the floors clean, doing the bulletins, fixing the facility, ushering, visitations, and child care are all opportunities for people to carry leadership responsibility and contribute to the overall success of their church.

Jesus set the pattern of leading by serving. We are on a journey to identify all of the opportunities to serve so that we can create a culture of servanthood. Tasks that seem insignificant are just as important to the overall success of a church as leading worship, playing an instrument, preaching the word, or any other ministry we could name. We need to honour all levels and encourage everyone to do the very best they can at each.

It is the responsibility of a manager to identify the levels of leadership in our midst. We cannot spend the same amount of time with each leader. Delegation becomes one of the vital abilities to master. The higher the level of your responsibility, the more defined your leadership sphere of influence. Most leadership training courses teach that twenty percent of people will take up eighty percent of your time. As an organization grows, we have to make some relationship decisions. I take the eighty-twenty principal and turn it around. If twenty percent of the people will take up eighty percent of my time, they need to be the top twenty percent, the fruitful workers in the church. If I allow my time to be used up by nonproductive people, it robs us in two ways: they don't achieve anything, and by using up my available time and energy, they limit or stop me from accomplishing my goals also.

I teach all levels of leaders to work themselves out of a job. This means that we are constantly redefining ourselves, delegating what we now embrace, and grabbing hold of a whole new role complete with new skills, relationships, and challenges. We cannot possess the new if we will not let go of the old. Our fear is that others do not have the maturity or skills developed or the understanding to do the job as well as we can. This is usually not just fear, but reality. Others probably don't know the task as well as you do, but that doesn't mean you cannot work yourself out of a job. It starts with an attitude that we are stewards, not owners of the title we now hold. We need to see change as an opportunity to grow and experience new things. New levels mean change. What got you to where you are is not going to get you to where you want to go. If you do not have anyone who can start to carry the responsibility for you, build a team. Break the task down into smaller parts and train two or three leaders—more, if necessary—to carry the responsibility together. By doing this, you are making room for others and positioning yourself for more opportunity. If there is only one who is available and they can only carry thirty percent of the responsibility, give it to them. This at least frees up thirty percent of your time, which allows you to expand your influence or increase your involvement in another area by the same ratio.

When we delegate, there will be mistakes made. I taught the mistake line principle in *The Power to Effect Change.* We should never use a mistake as a ceiling to opportunity. If someone is giving their best, they will make some mistakes. As long as they aren't making the same mistakes over and over again, they will eventually become good leaders. The mistakes are a sign that they are reaching their level of leadership experience. We should use the mistake as an opportunity to equip, not just correct. When a mistake is made, it should be seen as a platform by which to train for future success.

Every member of your church is a leader. They may not be leading a church program, but in their sphere of influence in the city, they are still leading someone, by their ability, charisma, money, or any form of relational influence. Everyone is leading someone, somewhere! Every area of life is about leadership or the lack thereof! If we do not aggressively provide leadership at all levels, it will create a void, and that void will get filled so that people are led by someone, to go somewhere.

The goal of an effective small town mega church leader is to maximize the resources it has in the house. We should never underestimate the potential of what we have in the church at any given time. I was watching a guest minister preaching one Sunday morning in our church. He was a very high-energy preacher and I knew he was going to get thirsty before he was done his message. I could see a bottle of water our staff had placed on the shelf on the pulpit, but I wasn't sure he knew it was there. A thought struck me at that moment—We can have a need, and the solution can be within arm's reach, but if we don't see it, we can miss the provision and live in the lack. We have to determine the assets that are within our grasp.

To do this, I would suggest that all churches do an all-inclusive asset assessment. Make an all-inclusive list of the skills and abilities in the congregation. List the intellectual power you have in the church. Are there any doctors? Lawyers? Accountants? Teachers? How about the intellectual power of everyday life? Are there those who are wise with money? Raising children? Marriage? Mechanical problems? Electrical problems? Welders? Any other skill or knowledge? List them all. Many times, a church has all the knowledge and skill needed to fulfill its calling sitting in the seats every week, but it hasn't defined a vision to gather, match, and embrace the collective strength.

As you do your assessment, list all other giftings—such as hospitality, those with strong work ethic, business skills, or any others you can think of. Be as complete as possible. We even identified some people who dress up as clowns and do parties for kids. Determine who you will go to for the gift of wisdom. There are those who carry wisdom in different areas. Identify people's strengths. In 2 Chronicles 14:5, we read how King Asa fortified his cities during times of peace. Conducting an asset assessment has the same intent. The more complete your assessment, the more able you will be to face the next challenge or obstacle you need to overcome. God knows what you need in your future and He will position people around you in advance ... if you pay attention.

There are those who have influence beyond title or position. I call these our bell heifers or pied pipers. They are the ones who people like to follow no matter where they are going. They tend to be successful or charismatic or both. In the days of cattle drives, cowboys would recognize a heifer that would wander off the path and lead half the herd in the wrong direction. They would put a bell on its neck. They knew that if they kept that heifer on track, the others would follow. A bell heifer is an incredible asset to the church, even if they are not leading a department. They are still leading the people. Bring them into the planning and they become very helpful in keeping the church on track and in unity.

There are those who are natural connectors and caregivers. I love these people. By their nature, they just engage people. When they become part of the Life Connection Team, they are some of the most valuable members of the church. Their ministry gives a "hands-on" personal touch to everyone.

The goal of the pastors in training ladder is to equip potential leaders with a broad knowledge of church responsibilities. We tend to focus on the five-fold giftings of apostle, prophet, evangelist, pastor, or teacher, but we are weak at another dimension that I call "Jesus CEO." Our future churches will manage well if they are well-managed! Our number one goal is to facilitate success.

I have already covered in the training ladder what we consider to be the eighteen key areas of ministry that people need to master in order to be considered candidates for senior staff positions. As the church matures and grows, there are a lot of other ministries to develop. The youth will split into different age groups—preteen, mid-teen (ages thirteen to sixteen), and then young adults (between seventeen to twenty-five). You will need people working with young couples, men's and women's ministries, and small groups of all kinds.

The following is a list of key pillar areas at the core of any functioning church, and the minimum number of people needed to keep each one going.

1. Pastoral Care – Three people.
2. Youth Ministry – Three leaders.
3. Kids Ministry – Five involved.
4. Worship – As many as possible, but a five-member team starts to have great service impact.
5. Prayer – Three prayer leaders, to cover the main departments of prayer (spiritual warfare, family, and city intercession teams).
6. Ushers – We could get by with three ushers for a season of time.
7. Social functions (such as planning fun events or preparing coffee after services) – Three people per function.
8. Life Connection Team – At least three concerned with follow-up and the integration of new people.

We see that it takes at least twenty-nine people to cause a church to start functioning properly.

It takes that many workers just to cover the key pillar functions of the church. If we don't have twenty-nine leaders, some of the existing core will have to wear many hats. That is why it takes passion and lots of hard work to build a new local church. This list gives you an idea of the minimum strength you need in a core group to even think of launching a new church. Until this kind of strength is achieved, or at least has potential, it is much better to remain as home groups with the intent of becoming a church plant. If you launch too soon, without core strength, even the most willing volunteers will be overwhelmed with the work load before long.

NINE

OVERCOMING GROWTH PLATEAUS

There are predictable and relatively consistent growth plateaus that can become barriers, or at least periods of flatline growth, to the new church plant. They are found when attendance hits 50, 125, 250, 500, 750, and upwards.

We need to understand the phases of the life cycle of a church instead of taking a snapshot of a period in time and assuming that all success will fall into the same pattern forever. The vision should remain consistent, but the expression is always being modified and improved to keep with the trends of the community. A church in most small towns would encounter a huge change if a factory or entity was started in the community that attracted multicultural workers. That church would have to shift its expression to engage the present trend while not compromising its original vision.

A breakout in church growth in an individual department can also cause the atmosphere and expression of a church to change. If the church was established with a strong kids ministry, a revival could break out in the youth in five to ten years as the kids who were raised in the vision hit their teen years. In this circumstance, the expression of the church would shift to accommodate what the Lord was doing at that present time.

There are many scenarios that alter the atmosphere and expression of a church, but the core values and vision needs to remain intact. It's important to determine the life cycle of the present trend. You can choose to believe that the present trend will last for generations, or you can develop a system that embraces and even creates future change.

All churches should plan for their death in three to five years. By this, I don't mean that this is the full extent of their life or that the leadership should be changed. What I mean is that churches should allow their emphasis and programs to have a natural life cycle and be intentional about change—every three to five years. My dad always says, "The only thing consistent in life is change," and I agree. Things will change whether we want them to or not, so we are far better off being intentional about it by building change into our strategy. Change happens either by intention or by default, but it will happen.

A healthy church embraces and receives change as a positive experience. An insecure church will try to defend the status quo and try to do what it has always done while expecting different results, simply because it has shouted it louder or is working harder. As most of us already know, this is the definition of insanity! This church is heading for a change in spite of its resistance, but the change will be much harder for everyone to accept or reposition for. This usually ends in relationship offences, and even church splits.

I believe a healthy tree is a tree that is nurtured and pruned on a regular basis. This applies to a church as well. Change may offend some, and even cause some to leave, but it is far better to allow some minor pruning along the way than to have a major split five years down the road when default change is forced.

Churches do change over time and we need to build fluid leadership teams that will not only meet the need, but help to create the change. A static leadership structure will become rigid as it defends the status quo. This structure will actually reject change until the change becomes stronger than the structure, at which time the structure will break.

A small town mega church must be able to recognize community trends and be aware of the growth barriers or plateaus. This must be understood in order to stay ahead of and take advantage of change as we proactively adjust our leadership teams. Each growth plateau demands that changes are made in leadership dynamics, emphasis ministries, roles, relationships, and responsibilities of the staff and team members. This creates a need for continued leadership development and skill training.

The list of things that change is almost endless, but there are a few things we should pay special attention to, or emphasize, at each level. A church will plateau or even reduce down to match the leadership dynamic used. Many will plant a new church through marketing and crusades. This will gather a group of people, but the leadership quality and dynamic will be the determining factor in how many actually stay to build the church. A leadership dynamic of one hundred and twenty-five will not keep a crowd of two hundred.

LEADERSHIP DYNAMICS AND ISSUES COMMON TO ALL LEVELS

1. Delegating
2. Relationships
3. Team building
4. Vision casting
5. Momentum
6. Creating a culture
7. Leadership
8. Personal development
9. Communication
10. Worship: matching skill and anointing
11. Conflict resolution
12. Crisis management
13. Integration of new people
14. Excellence
15. Accountability and transparency
16. Administration
17. Training
18. Synergy
19. Alignment of vision in all departments and initiatives
20. Outreach: effective community engagement
21. Development of key departments and programs for each level

22. Marketing: internal and external messaging
23. Creating vision *and* maintenance strategies for ages and departments
24. Developing common user-friendly language
25. Social programming

In the early stages of development, when church attendance is **below fifty people**, we are in the start-up phase. This stage of church planting can have different dynamics relevant to the culture you are in. My cousin planted churches in northern Italy for many years, and in that region the born-again churches where very small. The ratio of believers to the population base was about one in ten thousand people. In this cultural dynamic, a church of fifty or sixty people was considered a success. This can happen in North America as well if you are in a small town or a cultural region that isn't or hasn't been evangelised yet. This is why we need to develop our own gauges of success.

I will cover this in further detail later, but in principle we need to know who we are trying to reach and why. If you are called to a small town or a specific people group or need in a community of any size, you may not be able to gauge your success by numbers. My point is that I understand that the growth plateaus are painting the picture with a broad brush, but in general the dynamics of leadership and the atmospheres we create remain fairly consistent. I know of many churches that are small in number but are doing a great work with specific people groups, or are meeting a specific need and are having a huge impact in their communities.

In the body of Christ, we tend to honour leaders by numbers rather than by obedience to their calling. Those who may be leading a small work, but are having big impact, deserve honour as well.

During the first growth plateau, the pastor is a hands-on leader. He or she will be involved in one way or another with just about everything that happens in the church. We tend to believe that running a small church would be easier than a church of four or five hundred, but in actual fact the pastor has to work harder when the church is small. He or she has to be the jack of all trades... and master of enough of them to have credibility. They have to set up and tear down, greet everyone, lead worship, do the announcements, prepare the bulletins, answer all calls, visit everyone in need, sweep the floor, and take out the trash! The pressure is also on them to preach like the best TV evangelist, heal the sick, prophesy with accuracy, sing like an angel, and cast out every devil that comes their way. They are really the super heroes of faith! This is why many will not plant a new work or why some that do will tell you that they will never do it again. As a church grows, people with skill and ability come as well and start to carry some of the load.

My wife Kim and I have been involved in twelve or thirteen church plants so far. In the early stages of church planting, the pastor is also the gatherer. I think the number one quality of a small church pastor is personality and a genuine love of the ministry and the people God has given to them. It is a very personal environment and deep relationships are forged that can last a lifetime. These can be great times, as the conversations are usually around vision, with an expectancy of what the Lord might do this time around. There tends to be many people who come to the Lord in the early stages of a church plant, because it is such a relational environment. I am always watching for opportunities to meet and connect with new people. At this stage, social functions are easy to arrange in any backyard, which feeds the relationship-based strength of the church. If people don't like you when they meet you at a barbeque, they probably won't like you behind the pulpit either! We can't hide behind a crowd or a staff when we are this small. We are living in a fishbowl and inviting people to join us.

While it is almost unavoidable that we use a hands-on approach to our leadership at this stage, we should always be preparing for the next growth level. We shouldn't wait for it to arrive. Learn to delegate, even if you have the time to do something yourself. We think we can do it ourselves until we get too busy, but in reality the habit of doing it ourselves, and the expectancy developed in the people that we will do things for them, is what causes us to try working harder to keep up with the growth demands of the church. The fact is that sooner or later, the growth stops at the level of leadership you are providing.

Many times, I work with pastors who are looking for a devil to blame for the attendance going up and down, but if you take a look at the reality, you will find that the average attendance is a reflection of the growth plateau that the church is in, which is created by the leadership dynamic they are using! This is why crusade-style church planting tends only to work if the one doing the crusade is the one who is going to pastor the new work. Many who attend a dynamic crusade come to the planted church afterward expecting the same level of ministry, and if it is not at the same level or dynamic, they won't stay. This leadership dynamic is also why church growth will plateau at about fifty or sixty people. There is only so much one person can do until their time is used up and it is tangibly impossible to fit any more work into their schedule. Working harder will only burn out the pastor, not grow a church. Many burn out and never break the first barrier because they try to work harder instead of working smarter. At this stage of church growth, the key areas to focus on are relationship building, social functions, outreach, vision casting, and core development. This includes finding willing helpers to work with you to run the core departments of the church and, through the process, identifying potential leaders.

DEVELOP THE CORE CULTURES

1. Worship
2. Kids
3. Youth
4. Ushers and greeters
5. Prayer
6. Social functions

Financial pressures are huge during this stage of church planting unless you are one of the fortunate ones who are sponsored by a larger organization, complete with salaries and benefit packages. This actually is quite normal for a church plant, but it usually comes with time limitations. Many get sponsored for six months or a year, after which they are on their own. Most pastors who are planting a new church work during the day. This is certainly possible for a season, but it doesn't take long before the demands of even a small crowd make it a huge challenge for a working man. I am always on the lookout for ways to help those who are doing a good work but are in an environment of limited resources. I haven't found the answer yet, beyond some potential opportunities in multi-level marketing, but it concerns me that people will start to see us as salesmen instead of pastors. Financial limitations make it hard to do effective advertising, buy good quality equipment, or rent high quality facilities. Small church pastors are usually stuck in survival mode. I take the approach of short-term pain for long-term gain. I suffer in some areas of my life to put as much strength as I possibly can into the things that will grow the church.

The next growth plateau you will reach is around **one hundred and twenty five people**. I think I like this stage of new church plants the best. At this stage, the new church will start to stabilize and can shift its focus to identifying those who are energizing the congregation. From here, it can start to build its core leadership team. We need to identify leaders and delegate some responsibilities to them that match their gifting and strength. A pastor who will not delegate due to lack of confidence in the people around him, or who has created a sense of purpose by personally performing the tasks, will develop a martyr mentality and become the limiting factor to church growth. In order to break this barrier, we must shift from hands-on leadership to team building and delegation. The initial emphasis is on the team leaders, but as soon as the leaders are competent, we must help them build the teams necessary to accomplish the tasks at hand.

Leadership development becomes the number one focus. If we cannot mentor, inspire, and impart to leaders, we cannot break this barrier. At this point, you should start to form consensus-driven leadership teams. This adds to creativity, but also starts the process of transfer of ownership of the vision. I don't look for total agreement; a general sense of well-being is sufficient.

Keep in mind the three conditions we use for new leaders:

1. They must be into the vision of the church (which means the vision is already defined).

2. They are a regular financial contributor to the church (if they are not faithful with financial support, they will not be faithful with ministry responsibility either)

3. They are in right relationship with other team members.

At this stage of church growth, I would spend eighty percent of my time with those who are leading or have the potential to lead. This means that we are already going to spend less relationship building time with the congregation. Some don't like the separation and will actually war against church growth so that they can go back to having close relationships with the pastor. Don't let your heart get in the way! Press forward and pour your life into those who are fruitful. Many churches don't break the first barrier because the pastor cannot let go of the intimate relationships that are, in fact, non-productive. An attempt to treat everyone with equal time, attend every event, conduct every personal visit, and be everybody's friend will not only use up a pastor's time, but also rob him of the quality time he needs to spend with new or potential leaders. In this scenario, new leaders eventually feel ignored or make mistakes, which causes many of them to give up or become discouraged, feeling that nobody appreciates their efforts. Spending a lot of time with non-productive people burns out the pastor and discourages potentially strong leaders from even trying. The church will return to the size of the leadership dynamic provided, no matter how hard you work. The pastor must identify, connect with, and impart the vision to the key leaders. This takes lots of time and energy, but is worth every second. It may seem like we are not growing as fast as we should, but even if more people came, we wouldn't engage and accommodate them properly until our leaders are in place. It is far better to focus on leadership training and team building and let the church grow as a by-product of the effective ministry and services it offers.

Volunteers are always important, and at this stage we should be nurturing a culture of servanthood. Identify and promote every opportunity to serve, from sweeping a floor to foreign missions. Volunteer appreciation gatherings and recognition are great ways to say thanks and to encourage others to help. The leaders you are mentoring can help to manage all the volunteers, and through the process they can start to build their own relationship-based teams.

The pastor must discipline himself to delegate responsibility to the other leaders and then help them manage their departments and build their teams. Keep in mind that a department head or team leader is doing it on your behalf; they are not given ownership without guidance or input from the pastor. The word *manage* means to care for something for someone else. The leaders are representing you and need to keep you fully informed and allow you to have input into their areas of responsibility, otherwise they will eventually lead their people in a different direction, which can split the church. Relationship is still the strongest glue to hold things together, but you cannot have relationship with everyone, so focus eighty percent of your time with the top twenty percent of your people—the fruitful people! The congregation must be taught and nurtured to receive ministry from people other than the pastor. This is the stage of growth that, if done well, will start to create strong momentum. More on momentum is coming up soon.

There are two measurements to monitor at this stage. The first is the overall attendance and the other is the core number of people who buy into the church and vision. You can hear it in their words as they start to talk about what "we" can or should do rather than telling the pastor what "he" could or should do. They use terms like "our" church rather than "your" church. Many times, we see the church attendance numbers stay relatively the same for a season of time, but the congregation eventually shifts from those who were just checking you out to those who have bought into the vision. This shift is just as important, and maybe in some ways even more important, than the numbers themselves. Continue to strengthen the core so that the inner strength grows at the same rate as the outer attendance.

As the congregation grows, the integration of new people becomes a little harder. That is, until the pastor has enough leaders trained to free up his time, or enough skill and experience to connect with the newcomers on his behalf. Don't let this stage discourage you. Stay focussed on training leaders, building the teams, and engaging new people as best as you can. If your biggest problem is the inability to connect with new people, you are on a winning track by training more leaders... because you will eventually build a team to address that need, and the success rate of new people staying in the church will increase.

The relational social functions are always at the core of building the church, but the focus of the pastor starts to shift. At this stage, most of his or her time is spent on those leading or potential leaders. This includes social time. The real glue or strength of a church is relationship, and it takes lots of time to develop bonds.

There is no such thing as wasted time if you are doing it together with your team members. At this stage, the pastor's time is given to the leaders, but a leader's time needs to be given to the people in their departments. As they spend time together sharing the vision, having fun, and working for the Lord, their team will naturally start to form. It is at this stage that all department leaders must have the ability to explain and promote the vision of the church, describe the structures and strategies, the statement of faith, the core values, and the actions we are taking to embrace the season of time we are in.

During this season, the church starts to have more management-type meetings. A lot of the communication and momentum building can be done through small groups. We start to develop life houses or home groups as we grow through this stage, as well as ministry training sessions for those who are interested. It is important to think through the desired church program dynamic at this time. When the church is about one to two hundred people, there are not enough members to warrant all programs. If you have a mid-week church service running and you start your home groups, you will find that many will start to choose one or the other. This is natural and will create strength when you have enough people to make both mid-week services and home groups effective. If you are still close to the one hundred members level, you will find that home groups will have a great impact on your mid-week attendance. You have to decide what you are trying to do and develop your program strategy accordingly.

We initially chose to make leadership and ministry development a high priority at this stage. We use our mid-week service to give platform to new ministries. We train new worship leaders, musicians, preachers, and specialty ministries during this service. This gives them a chance to develop their calling, and it gives us a chance to know their strengths and weaknesses. We critique the preachers and ministries and give them positive feedback for greater impact. We found that trying to run home groups at the same time actually warred against the mid-week service success. We don't try to run mid-week service and home groups until we are around two hundred members or more.

I am not trying to make an argument against home groups—they may work very well for you. I am simply trying to point out how important it is to determine your program choices at this stage. You may love home groups, but if you don't know the home group leaders very well, you may not feel comfortable having them teaching and ministering to the congregation members at this point. Personally I like to get to know potential leaders in a public setting before allowing them to lead a department or private small group. We use the mid-week service to this end. When we get to know and trust so many ministries and leaders that we can no longer fit them in and give them platform in one mid-week service, we start to add home groups. This has worked well for us so far, but every church needs to determine what program flow best fits their leadership dynamic. As long as you are working towards equipping and releasing leaders, you will eventually build a strong team.

No matter what program strategy you choose, the interest may be small at first. At times, you may only be working with one or two people in a certain area of ministry, but don't be discouraged; pour your life into the one or two, and then reproduce them. This process will produce fruit if you stay on track with patience and determination. Leaders should spend time defining what material, message, and programs are needed to bring clarity, focus, and strength for the season of time the church is in and how it connects to the long-term vision. All small groups should connect people to the vision and the pastors. They are not going to help if they are off on their own special interest or direction. If they have another vision, it eventually brings *di*vision. A leader of a department that does not agree with or will not align to the greater vision and purpose of the church should not be leading, no matter how much you like them or how gifted you think they are. If they are well liked and gifted, but heading in another direction, they are really gathering momentum to build their own church or are functioning with an Absalom spirit that is undermining the effectiveness of the rest of the leadership team. It comes out in words like, "If I was making the decision," "If it was me," or "The pastor means well, but…" If this kind of attitude develops in any department, it is only a matter of time before an issue arises that will justify their perspective. They will then try to overthrow the present pastors and leaders, or if they are not able, they will split the church. The best way to war against this kind of failure is by spending time with your leaders, including them in the decision-making process as much as possible, and doing all you can within the vision to facilitate their success.

By the time the church is around one hundred and twenty-five people, it should be able to determine its natural inherent strengths. Every church tends to attract people of like faith, and we need to pay attention to who has connected to us and why. By doing so, we can match the programs we offer with the strength of our teams. Through this process, it becomes quite easy to identify the limitations of our team, the obstacles and challenges we need to overcome, and the leaders and teams that need to be built. This gives our core leadership teams something to work on as they develop strategies to overcome each limitation or weakness. Pastors do not have to be the ones with all the answers; they just have to be wise enough to find those who do.

I think this is why I like this level of church planting the best; we are spending a lot of time talking vision and determining possibilities. At this stage of the church plant, there are a lot of options, so we tend to have lots of brainstorming sessions with every department, with every age engaged as much as possible. This is where a consensus-driven decision-making process starts to develop. As I said earlier, I don't necessarily seek total agreement. Instead, a sense of well-being should prevail. In the book of Acts, the early church debated issues until it seemed good to them and the Holy Spirit, and then they wrote guidelines. This is a very good way to govern a church.

The emphasis added at this stage is:

- The pastor's time shifts to leaders.
- Strategies for the next season are developed by consensus of the team.
- Small groups start to develop.
- Delegation becomes a vital skill for the pastors.
- Communicating to the teams and people becomes more of a challenge and a higher priority.
- A corporate synergy or collective strength starts to develop in order to produce a product that is greater than the sum of its parts.
- The church leadership dynamic starts to shift to a

greater team emphasis.

- The pastor now needs to grow faster than the church. The skill sets now needed change from hands-on meeting the needs of the people, to the mentoring, resourcing, and coaching of leaders and teams.

The next growth plateau is hit after about **two hundred and fifty people.**

This stage is possibly one of the hardest barriers to break through. It requires almost everything to shift. The senior pastors are now even farther removed from the day-to-day engagement of the people and the ministry load starts to fall on a corporate management team. This is a hard shift because the ones who did the ministry work to build the church to this level now have to disengage from the hands-on people care to spending eighty percent of their time developing department heads and their teams. The needs of the people start to be addressed by teams or departments in the church rather than the pastoral staff. Efficient and effective programming becomes the catalyst for church growth.

This is hard for some of the people to get used to, but I think it is even harder for the staff that has spent so long, in some cases years, building the church by spending time meeting the needs of the people. It is so hard to let go that in some cases the staff member may desire not to move into another leadership dynamic so that they can stay hands-on with the congregation. It is much better to do your best to accommodate this individual rather than force them to take on a role they really don't enjoy. Meeting the needs of the people never takes a backseat or becomes irrelevant, so if there are those who wish to stay in that role, it is a very good thing for the strength and level of care of the church. But in the end, regardless who takes on the role and responsibility of being a part of the management of the church, it needs to be done to continue to grow beyond this plateau.

I always encourage pastors, when putting together the church's legal board and management team, to include the people who are actually doing the work, leading a department, or carrying some significant responsibility. Many times, we have management teams or boards made up of people who are watching what is being done but not really doing anything themselves. To me it is like a beer-bellied, out-of-shape sports fan sitting in the bleachers shouting foul criticisms at the athletes for their mistakes and effort. I have learned that spectators are criticizers. The game looks a whole lot different when you are the one on the playing field! It gives you a lot more compassion and understanding for the other team members, allowing you to celebrate their success and be there to encourage them when they fail.

The church at this stage should be moving towards being compartmentalized. The leaders should start taking responsibility to organize and lead brainstorming sessions with their teams, developing strategies, determining budgeting needs, finding their own volunteers, creating momentum in their department, and bringing positive energy and attitudes into the church. This level of leader must be low maintenance, very loyal, and very productive in order for the church to continue to grow.

The dynamics of church leadership becomes less about skill sets or abilities to run a department in itself than it is about developing the skill of creating a culture. To manage a department, by nature, implies that you are doing it on behalf of or under the instruction or guidance of another. This involves the management of resources, guiding the direction, dealing with conflicts, and all kinds of other management responsibilities.

To create a culture, another skill set is needed. Leaders must be able to clearly define and promote the vision for their department or initiative. The goal is to promote and integrate their strength into the other departments of the church. Prayer can start by being its own department, but at this stage it needs to become a common strength of all departments. A youth department should now become actively engaged in all departments of the church. If we want to engage youth, we must create a culture they will want to come in to. If we want stronger prayer, we must create a culture where prayer is the life flow of all we do. If we want evangelism, we don't need an evangelistic department that stands alone; we need a department that is creating a culture of evangelism by equipping the saints for the work of the ministry. Every department should shift from a stand alone initiative to the development of a church-wide culture that reflects its area of responsibility.

At this stage, we need to start putting all of our materials, strategies, and tracking systems into print with feedback reports and information on the status and health of each department. It is impossible to keep the church all heading in the same direction by the old methods of one-on-one or small group meetings. We need to articulate and clearly market what is happening, why it is happening, who is leading, what the needs are, and where it will take us. The more effective our communication, the more we can create and maintain momentum and efficiency.

The emphasis added at this stage:

- Leadership teams shift from managing a responsibility to integrating their strength into all departments.
- All roles, relationships, and responsibilities are clarified and redefined.
- There is greater internal marketing and communications.
- There is more team building and vision casting sessions.
- All programming is updated to improve effectiveness and efficiency.
- The emotions caused by the disengagement of pastors from the people are dealt with. (How do you keep pastors interactive with the people with a minimum amount of time?)
- Everything starts to be put in print.

At the **five hundred plus** stage of church development, leadership roles are established and, as far as I can tell, don't change a lot no matter how large the church eventually becomes. Many become the face or personification of the corporation. This works very well for those with charismatic personalities, especially if they are doing television broadcasts. Whether the senior pastor does the work of the CEO of the church, or he/she has become the corporate image and marketing focus of the ministry, doesn't change the fact that someone is doing the CEO job. At this point, senior staff roles are defined and remain fairly consistent in continued growth as far as the function is concerned. The CEO must do just that: be the chief executive officer. This means that their primary role has shifted away from program application, or the actual engaging or leading of the church, to one of governance. At this level, there are many philosophy type issues to address. By this, I mean how theology is applied in the church. They are responsible for the big picture issues that steer and build the church. They deal with the overall budget targets and building plans. They work with management teams to determine the flow for the next season of time and how to expand and market the church without losing personal care. Very few pastors at this level, at least the ones I have met, actually do the day-to-day weddings, funerals, or visitation type work of the pastoral ministry. This, of course, varies relative to the size of the church. At five hundred, you will still see senior pastors engaging the people, but after one thousand, the transition becomes more obvious. You would more likely find them having meetings with a TV station, building committees, or steering the administration department. Men and women at this level tend to be great motivators, team builders, and vision casters. Success at this level allows for the church to double in growth before another growth barrier is reached.

By the time you have reached the **seven hundred plus** stage, your church programming is usually defined and fairly polished. The leadership teams have matured to a place of success and the facility or budget issues are taken care of by those with financial experience. At this level, the experienced leaders that are contributing to the vision bring a higher degree of accuracy in decision-making and the wisdom available is far beyond what a church of one hundred could ever hope for. This increase in corporate capacity increases the odds of even greater success. A church of this size has defined its calling, developed its unique expression, and has created the atmospheres that their people identify with. This creates a corporate image or identity. It usually comes complete with music style and dress codes (intentional or by default—it is human nature to conform to the image of our environment).

The main focus of effective ministry and continued growth is good management (through progressive communication, team building, and training programs, etc.). There is not usually a great need for new programs, as all the main areas tend to be fairly well covered by this stage. The challenge tends to be more in increasing efficiency, expanding the church's influence, and reproducing more of the same departments that are already in place. We may have been able to handle the pastoral care with one team in the past, but now due to the size and demand on our time, we have to develop another team. Another leader is chosen and another team is built. We start to delegate specific functions to each team like visitations or counselling, while others may designate regions of the city, age groups, or specific needs of the region. There are many ways to address the issue of reproduction of services and there isn't one that is better than the others. We all need to develop the best way of reproducing our present effective teams in a way that works for us. What worked for someone else may be cumbersome and confusing to our team.

I was told many years ago that as a church grows, it should not stop doing what made it great in the first place. We don't have to drop all of our ways and adopt what someone else has done; we just need to reproduce what we know works for our leaders and teams. It comes down to each management team member effectively carrying specific responsibilities in the congregation, or to the community, on behalf of the church.

I will let those who have built much larger churches than I have teach us how it is done. They are much better equipped and experienced to address the issues facing larger churches. The purpose of this book is to inspire ideas in those who haven't reached the level where resources and staff are readily available.

At all levels, I work at establishing what I call "bookends." We define the reality of where we are at on the one end, and place our goals on the other. This bookend concept triggers our creative minds as soon as we see the gap between the two ends. God has given us a natural ability to see obstacles as soon as we know where we are at present and where we want to get to. As soon as the goal is established, our minds instantly start making lists of all the reasons why we can't get there. We tend to let this discourage us, because we can see so many obstacles. We can feel overwhelmed and give up before we give it a genuine try. I have learned to embrace the list that my mind makes when facing a challenge and then use it as a guideline for achievement. If you will just write out the list as it comes, you will find that your mind has just taken the big problem and broken it down into individual parts. Now that you have smaller individual parts to deal with, you can develop a strategy to address each one. As each one is strategically addressed, you can move forward towards your goal until you have overcome all limitations and totally achieved or exceeded your objectives. Every church of every size has its challenges and obstacles to overcome, but you can use the bookend formula as a tool to help make what seems like an overwhelming, impossible task a little easier to face.

TEN

JOINING STRENGTH AND WISDOM

The greatest thing we can do for our children is create an environment where they enjoy coming to church. McDonalds knew how to create generational customers. We can learn from their success. A child that grows up thinking church is good, has some fun, and builds some friendships will grow up connected to the local church. We have developed a life flow strategy to include all ages. Children up to their teenage years are taught the "principles of"... the principles of life, the principles of leadership, of faith, of money, of relationships, of God, and of vision. When they become teenagers, and especially at about sixteen or seventeen, we want them to learn how to use the principles in real life situations. We then move them into the "experience of" season of their lives. We embrace them in the leadership of the church. We don't just use them as slaves; we allow them to have direction-setting input in all we do—the color schemes and decor of the church, the music, the service flow, the people care, the administration, and the training of teams. They learn leadership skills, vision casting, and team building. We teach them conflict resolution, management skills, and marketing techniques, as well as exposing them to many other character and skill development circumstances. They are very visible during the services and have their own Friday night youth church to manage.

We focus a lot of our relationship attention on the seventeen to twenty-five year olds. This age group has the youthful zeal and personality to connect with the younger teens and preteens. They are the role models, mentors, or big brothers and sisters. They are also mature enough to spend time with the older generation in the church. They play a very important role in eliminating the generation gap. When we chart the strategy on a bell curve, we see that the peak, or our greatest emphasis, is on this age group. This does not at all mean that the other ages are not wanted or not valuable to the success of the church. After all, the older generation also has an important role to play. When recorded on a bell curve, it ramps up from one to sixteen years old. The centre or peak of the bell curve represents the involvement of the young people as they get practical real life experience in the church. As they reach their early to mid-twenties, they are faced with career choice, post secondary education, marriage and family, and many other issues of life. These real life issues tend to limit the time they have available to be at the church. The bell curve drops to reflect their changing role or their reduced time commitment. They need to be released to their life choice but continue to be mentored.

This is where the older, more life seasoned generation plays a very important role. They are the mentors, councillors, and encouragers to those who are stepping out into life. Some need help to start careers, businesses, or political or educational roles. They also need guidance with practical life skills, like how to handle finances or raise a family. What an opportunity for our older and experienced generation! The younger, emerging generation shouts for joy when those with life skill and experience spend time with them.

We can teach in five years what took us twenty-five years to learn. The focus of the small town mega church isn't about the success of the church—it's about "how" the church succeeds! We tend to pass on what we have accomplished instead of mentoring the next generation in the process of discovery and transition.

Life is about change. We are a transitional people. The world changes at an incredible rate and the church needs to be out front of the coming trends. The expression of success may change, but the principles of success remain fairly consistent.

There are many things to pass on to the next generation, but I'm going to assume that you can make a great list on your own that would include knowledge of the word, their gifts or character, and morality. I want to focus for a moment on the coming trends I see.

ELEVEN

THE TRENDS I SEE

John Lennon once said that the world is changing with or without us. I don't know if he realized just how true that statement was. In his day, the music world was making an impact on the social dynamics of North America. The music expressed the tensions of the political and social climates of the era. It was helping to create the context for change and was the beginning of the unknown future.

During those years, society was driven by a status quo value system that defined cultural identity. This image was expressed and reinforced in most mediums. TV shows where governed by accepted moral codes. Even the swinging hips of the young rocker Elvis Presley was too much for the viewers of his day. But change was in the wind. We could spend time analyzing each event in the recent one hundred or more years to acknowledge their contribution to what we call normal today. But for the purposes of this discussion, I would like us to put these events into the context of some greater and longer term historical trends.

We are caught in a season of one of the greatest mega trends in social culture in the last three to four hundred years.

We tend to focus on the trends of the last century, with the shift from an agricultural-driven economy, with its core values of family and a sense of safety in community—a time when inheriting the family farm was the goal of many young men. This was a time when hard work was not seen as a catalyst of success, but rather the necessity of survival. A sense of community was cherished, people knew their neighbours, local church was valued, church picnics brought families together, family dances were alcohol-free (and included the kids), and it was common for the community to respond to a barn-raising event just to help a neighbour. This era may have lacked in technology or medicine, but it did have some social strengths that are almost absent in our present culture.

Then we moved to the industrial revolution, where climbing the corporate ladder and material possession became the main gauge of success. Success was defined by possession, power, and fame. We held onto some of the social values, but the trend shifted from the family farm to the factory. Life became about the workplace rather than the family living room. The mindset shifted to work ethics, pension plans, and internal positions of prestige and power. Providing for the family was still important, but many times it came at the cost of being absent from it.

We then moved to the age of high-technology, where knowledge was power and the stock market was driven by speculation and overnight success stories. The information exchange and easy access to knowledge of any kind made the world seem smaller in some ways, and yet vast and overwhelming in others. In the information age, the main emphasis shifted from access to knowledge in and of itself to how knowledge was used. Self-help, how-to guides, and steps to achievement are part of the status quo language of today.

Although these eras all have distinct cultural dynamics, they still fall into one common denominator: they are all driven by the pursuit of "logic" and "reason." This means that mankind has "reason" as the basic platform or starting point in our thinking. In all of our efforts, we have developed a basic philosophy that man can break down any phenomenon, analyze the elements, and discover the principles of cause and effect, and through the process we are sure it will bring us to a clear solution—or at least an ability to understand and explain it all. This tendency in what we call the modern world is a part of a greater cultural dynamic, and we are once again on the verge of change!

Again the words of John Lennon ring true—the world is changing… with or without you!

Prior to the seventeenth century, society had a basic, accepted perspective that all things were controlled by the supernatural… we had to keep the gods happy. All life was judged by the interactions between man and the unknown, unseen gods. This created a sense of "wonder" and "fear" in the cultural dynamics of mainstream society. In the centuries that followed, science and philosophy became the mindset of the mainstream. Reason became the main pursuit of the unexplained. This created a cultural dynamic where the disciplines of science, philosophy, psychology, and even theology developed the ten steps to achievement, the four principles of life, and so on… all based on a premise that all things in life could be broken down into smaller parts that could be understood and applied by reason.

We are now in another shift in cultural mindsets. We are seeing a shift in the premise, or the starting point of understanding in itself, and it effects the way we view all other aspects of life. This shift is happening and will continue to happen with or without us. We are *not* going to see another cultural shift in the pattern of the last one hundred years with reason as the basic cultural mindset. *We are going to experience a change in the starting point of thought itself.* This shift is starting now and will continue for the next fifty years, with the highest transitional impact hitting us over the next fifteen years.

The context of thought over the last three hundred years has been that we could pursue knowledge and, through reason, we could overcome or at least explain any challenges life placed before us. Challenges were approached with a positive perspective and a confidence in our capacity to overcome. All problems and discussion were based on commonly accepted value systems that drew a line in the sand. With these social core values or ideals, we could debate opposing views, much like looking at the two sides of a coin. But at the core of the thought pattern was an ideal that we could identify the cause, define a clear solution, and develop guidelines to navigate the situation.

Now the mindset of society is shifting from positive "reason"… to a starting point of the "perceived impossible." The thought that anything can be broken down into definable absolutes has been rejected. Now discussion is becoming broader and more perspectives are being considered. It's no longer akin to debating the two sides of a coin, but rather more like placing a large beach ball in the centre of a room and each occupant giving his or her input of the truth they see from their perspective. The premise is that just because it is different from one person's experience or understanding doesn't mean it's wrong. There is a new core belief that if we are to gain any form of truth, we must include all of the perspectives and come to some sort of collective agreement which can be described as "relative," rather than "absolute" truth.

The starting point of discussion is shifting to a negative perspective that snubs its nose at past attempts to address life with reason, or that we could possibly reach an absolute truth through any means. This negative perspective refutes any attempt to claim that we can gain understanding of any issue of life from only one perspective, or that there is only one absolute answer to any question. Just as the pre-sixteenth century mindset of the gods created a sense of wonder or fear, and the later years of science and philosophy created one of reason... these years are creating a cultural mindset that I am naming... "experiential collective truth."

The truth now becomes relative to your situation and the cultural community you choose to be a part of. Truth is established by how I hear it or how I perceive it to be, but reinforced by the community I belong to. The gang, or sphere of relational community, is the new family of the twenty-first century. My gang, friends, church, or political party all reinforce what I perceive as truth, and this gives me a sense of belonging.

During the early years of wonder, all influences of life came from the outside-in. An individual was at the mercy of the gods or other supernatural elements beyond understanding of mere mortals. During the years of reason, life was explained and developed by self-awareness, which is a life controlled and developed from the inside-out. This perspective had some common core values and accepted absolutes. Now, the "starting point" of information exchange and knowledge transfer is "unbelief!" Truth is now relative to my circumstance and life experiences. The truth of any message is established by how the hearer receives it… not how the messenger delivers it.

Guidelines for life are established by "experiential collective truth." By this, I mean that all new information is brought into the existing values of the hearer's current life experience. These existing values have been created by their own perspectives and reactions to life-shaping events. These experiential values then get reinforced by the collective affirmation of a person's peer group.

Truth now becomes "relative"—not "absolute".

The sense of family, community, and purpose is established by the main core value of "belonging." In the face of uncertainty, we all withdraw to the familiar. The familiar may not be in the best long-term interests of the individual, but being embraced by the familiar creates a sense of security, commonality, and belonging. This has a stronger life force than family, faith, or fear of consequences. We get drawn into environments and relationships that reinforce our experience and the agreement of the peer group forms a collective, relative truth. This relative truth makes all truth "fluid," based on situations and circumstances. It is perceived as right based on experiential collective agreement. Anyone who challenges our collective truth must me wrong and would need to be changed, eliminated, or ignored as being out of touch with reality.

This all sounds pretty scary to the status quo mindset of reason and logic. We may even choose to avoid the issue, withdraw into our artificial culture of the familiar, or rise up in defiance, but in the end change will come with us or without us. The fear is generated from the unknown, and fear causes us to withdraw to the familiar.

What I propose is that we embrace the inevitable change that's before us. The change will happen willingly or by force... but it will happen. If we isolate ourselves out of fear or resistance, change will come by force. I propose that we embrace the opportunity to define history and make our mark as a generation of proactive people who understood the value of creating a synergy of strength for the common good of all.

This future strikes fear in our inner being like a sledgehammer striking a steel pillar. It shakes the very core of our existence. It should! The change that is before us should not be taken lightly, but at the same time, we should not be paralyzed by fear of the unknown or be reluctant to let go of the safety found in the familiar. The future has the potential to be the most creative and positive interactive time in the history of mankind. We fear a new paradigm of interaction because all we have known is the paradigm of the teacher-student—"I'm the boss, you're the employee. I'm the expert or the one in authority, so listen to me." When we try to bring this new paradigm into our everyday life, it changes so many of our familiar dynamics that we reject the thought that maybe we could create something that would be even better. Remember, just because it's familiar doesn't make it better!

You have already been influenced by experiential collective truth. What you perceive as truth today is a result of your upbringing, your education, your experiences, and your reactions to circumstances of life. We think we are on the right track because our social relationship group's mindset is relatively on the same page and we all can't be wrong. So our expression of truth is also an expression of experiential collective truth.

Again, change is on the horizon whether we want it or not. There is a reason why we can still listen to 1950s rock and roll on our radio stations across the land. The baby boomers are still in control of society. We have enough representation in the population to get our way. We can vote to get the political party of choice. We still maintain control of the financial world, so we have the power to build infrastructure and programming to accommodate our aging culture. For years, baby boomers have created and maintained what has become the status quo of every sector of society. Challenging this status quo has meant being identified by those with position and power as rebellious or uncooperative.

But this is the very thing that is changing. The status quo is not only being "challenged." It is being "replaced," whether we like it or not. There is a population base already birthed that can shift the collective powers. They are still children, but in the next fifteen years they will become the mainstream status quo. They will have the collective voting power, the majority influence on culture, and they will get their own way. The mindset of the baby boomers will be replaced.

In the corporate world or the workplace, we can resist the change and hold on to the familiarity of the status quo for the next twenty years. We may even survive that, but we will eliminate ourselves from being the innovative corporations we are today as the next generation's intellectual power gravitates towards corporate climates that embrace their collective truths and cultural ways.

Many would see this as a threat to the very fabric of our democratic capitalistic world. I would propose that it can make us even stronger, more creative, and better able to adapt to the ever-changing issues of rapid international integration.

Anyone who knows me has recognized that I have two main strengths in my life and ministry. The first is that I am a strategist. I think strategically about any problem or challenge placed before me. If you give me a circumstance, my mind races with possibilities. With this comes an inherent understanding of the seasons or times we are in. My second strength is an understanding of corporate team dynamics. It's from these two perspectives that I address the issue of engaging the next generation and embracing the point of change. We have already discussed some of the cultural trends of our immediate future, so now let's take a look at the structural dynamics of the coming age.

One of the main elements to a successful church, business, city, political party or to society at large is the governmental structures we create. During the era of reason, leadership of any corporate environment, from federal government to the local church, had a tendency to disengage the very people who supported their rise to power. This isn't done intentionally or out of some misguided conspiracy. It happens due to the systems, structures, and procedures we use. We have developed an "I'm the expert" mentality which says, "Bring me your problem and I will give you a solution. Listen and cooperate with my guidance and things will be well." As this mindset has become more prevalent in our culture, society at large has given over our lives' responsibility to institutions. It is now in the minds of many that it is the responsibility of government to look after me, the workplace to cater to my desires, the schools system to educate my children, and the church to teach about ethics in life or the reality of God. It feeds a mindset that the world owes me, so I don't have to put much effort into it. This mindset allows us to be armchair critics who only have to judge the efficiency of the institution without having any ownership of its well-being. It says that if my kids aren't doing very well, it's societies fault. If they are bored, society should build something to entertain them. If they are hungry, we should feed them, and at all costs we should never tell them they are wrong. This is one of the main factors of tension in the workplace. We aren't dealing with just a lack of work ethic; we are dealing with a mindset created by our experiential collective truth. The younger generation was raised in a mindset of institutionalized responsibility over individuals. I believe that the workplace is the greatest environment to address this social issue. In the workplace, we have a vested interest in pursuing synergy to produce a better product in a very competitive world. I am working to develop training materials to aid us in shifting corporate culture.

All corporate cultures have a history of development and discovery that has defined who they are today. There are many stories of corporate development, but within these stories we find a common growth pattern that we need to recognize as part of the process that embraces or rejects change.

In the early stages of any new initiative, we have an excitement and an energy created by anticipation. This sense of adventure connects with the frontier spirit at the core of human nature. The new initiative seems to run on pure adrenalin for a season of time, which creates a buzz of excitement combined with a determination to succeed. This energy tends to attract more customers, which expands the vision and increases the potential. The success of the early stages of growth demands that we start to become better organized and more effective in regards to the programming and services we provide.

Once again, we see the pattern as we start to attract management oriented leaders. We get to a place where things are working well, but not growing anymore. We call in the experts, we go to conferences, and still we see no movement, so we blame the people—or devils—but in reality we should take a look at our structures within themselves. If we want to have a sustainable generational church or business, we have to structure in such a way that allows that to happen.

As we look at church history, we can see that it isn't normally devils or uncooperative people that kill a church movement. Nor is it always the economy that kills the continued success of a business. The movement dies as we start to defend the status quo systems and structures more than what motivated us to pursue it in the first place. By doing this, we keep any hope of fresh entrepreneurial energy from breaking out!

The former generation or status quo fights to defend its well-polished proven ways as the next generation feels totally unconnected, uninvolved, and uninterested in something that isn't relevant to their ways of doing things. So the first issue to address when you reach the point of change is "decentralized team dynamics." This shift towards engaging the masses transfers a sense of ownership to the employees of a corporation, the cultures within a city, the cities of a nation, and ultimately transfers our common values and connects with the next diverse generation. The problems are easy to identify and the answers are yet too abstract to define. So at this point, the question we should address is, *How do we engage these diverse cultures of the next generation?*

Now more than ever we will see that language is the main currency and sculptor of the new cultural mindset. If we hope to connect across the cultural, age, and psychological barriers, we need to become masters of communication. Over the last three hundred years, we have communicated in a point form, teacher-student atmosphere that says, "I have it figured out and you should listen to me if you want to succeed." The new language of communication is presented as a narrative… a story… much like Jesus with His parables in His day.

The new form of communication is not a set of absolutes wrapped up in a one-way only, take-it-or-leave-it package. We, the baby boomers, were able to use that kind of teaching approach because we had enough agreed upon common values and navigational forces to steer cultural dynamics. In this new era, we won't have the same leverage, so our decision-making will reflect more of a consensus-driven process. Those who follow cultural trends claim that the platform presentations of future generations won't take the form of a list of expert advice, but rather a contextual, principle-based narrative that connects to the imagination of the listener. In the former instructor-based presentations, we acquired knowledge complete with the application in a step-by-step format. This learning process required adherence to the steps of success, but required very little imaginative thought process. There was little need to pursue or even consider other possibilities. We tend to accept that the perceived expert has already considered the other options and rejected them as irrelevant or lesser in value. We accept that they have done the work to come up with the best option for our success. This has become the status quo process of communication and it has been driven by popular demand. This style of information gathering requires very little research or thought on the part of the listener. It is true that this approach is convenient, but it also opens a whole lot of opportunity for error. We make the assumption that the communicator is accurate and right.

The communication choice of the future will be done in more story form, or illustration-style teaching. We will still be providing our listeners with the values and principles we desire to convey, but at the same time our communication will allow the listener to process and engage the narrative the way he wants to, coming to his own life application conclusions.

Some see this as a step in the wrong direction, but Jesus used this approach as He spoke about eternal truths in the context of a life-relevant parable. Those who had an ear to hear... heard. This communication style does not mean vague dialogue that lacks any substance, or one that avoids proposing a clear position on any issue. We still need to communicate clear values. The communication shift isn't in the content; it's in the attitude of the presentation. The hearer doesn't want to be told what to do, but does need to hear what we stand for, so he or she knows if they are interested in becoming part of our relationship-based subculture community or group. If the hearer is in agreement with the narrative's values and cause, then that environmental truth will be accepted as the guideline, reinforced by experience and the affirmation of the peer group. So in order to communicate with the next diverse cultural generation, we need to proclaim our position with clear, definable, and consistent values. Slogans and marketing statements that reflect your corporate or collective mindset become not just an outreach statement, but the visual imagery and core beliefs that define and shape your internal culture. Truth is presented as a proposition from your perspective, or in the case of a Christian life, truth is presented as a propositional narrative from a biblical perspective. A propositional narrative *can be* made while still making clear statements of the biblical or collective values we hold as truth.

This new style of communication will force us to define our identity. The definable identity is what gives our people a sense of "belonging" to those who choose to accept our value system as truth.

This new culture will force us all to clearly define, communicate, and express openly who we are and what we represent! Imposters, wannabes, and program-oriented thinkers will be exposed and rejected very quickly. Collective language creates identity, which enhances familiarity and feeds the sense of belonging. Community "belonging" is the greatest core value of the future. Expressions of the future will need to clearly display this value of "community over individuality." This is a major shift, as the last three hundred years have promoted individuality. This goes back to my points on structures. A top-down disengaged leadership style will not connect with the next generation. Through decentralized corporate team dynamics, we can create opportunity and structures to engage the people, transfer ownership, and fuel their sense of belonging.

The greatest challenge of all this is that it isn't a line drawn in the sand that we simply cross over and are done with. It's a transitional process of change. We need to keep in mind that the old systems and mindsets are still the status quo of our culture and, at this point, still alive and well. My proposal is that we are reaching a *point* of change and we should educate ourselves as much as possible regarding what that change could look like. We should ask ourselves, how will we not only survive, but thrive in this new environment? How will we embrace the change? We need to develop a proactive and willing approach to change rather than the forced change brought on by ignorance or resistance.

The generation we are moving into is a generation where language is the key. From the Christian perspective, we already understand the concept that we are developed by language or words, Gods language ... His word! We would go so far as to say that we are even situated in life by a greater purpose that God had in mind before we were born. This means that when we are born, we have a reason to exist; we don't have to create one. We have guidelines for life found in the language of the Bible. Many of the life truths of scripture are hidden in narratives we call parables. We find we can read the same passage many times in our lives and each time get a greater, deeper, or totally new truth. These parables are narratives which hold such a depth and variety of truth that in a crowd of one hundred people, there could be one hundred separate yet accurate truths arrived at. These truths were contained in the narrative, but determined as a truth by the individual hearer and his or her life experiences.

Words have creation power. It is with our words that we create our own mini-culture, complete with its "life flow." We can use words to organize moral or ethical actions. We understand what's behind the words of the Pro Life movement. We recognize the slogans of social groups and their causes and we develop our own versions to call attention to ours. We use words to bring focus, attract attention, and get support for our cause. This approach has been very effective in the past due to the cultural mindset that says, "If we first draw attention to the problem, then analyze the root cause, we can develop or even become the solution to any problem."

This former cultural mindset has many starting points of thought. One thought is that we think any problem can be broken down into identifiable root causes, that life is explainable enough to understand if broken into smaller parts. We have also historically started with a mindset that is naïve enough to think that we can actually solve all problems. We are caught in a logic that says everything can and should be explained by cause and effect principles.

This positive, overcoming perspective is the core belief system that is being challenged by the next generation. The new communication has a predetermined awareness that all presentations are opinionated and tainted by the presenter's life experiences. This means that no matter how compelling the argument may sound, I am aware that I am only hearing one perspective on the subject, which may be channelled through a lens of experience that is completely irrelevant to my circumstance or cultural value system.

This endless circle of possibilities and perspectives creates a world where criticism becomes the accepted, and even expected, culture. This communication dynamic demands that I don't accept your concept and presentation of truth as the only absolute option. I must provide input from my experience in order to gain a broader and more inclusive perspective, and therefore a more complete understanding of the situation.

In this kind of environment, the development of common language becomes the catalyst for community. Common language can only be developed by engagement and agreement. Common language reflects a social consensus of the core values of a culture. If we don't pursue the common language to reflect our values, we will never achieve a sense of community and we will feed segregation and social tensions. If we do work on inclusive, consensus-style communication, I believe through common language we can create the sense of identity which becomes familiar to the individual and provides that crucial sense of belonging. We can actually embrace change rather than resist the inevitable.

In summary, I would propose this:

- We should work hard to engage and integrate the next generation.
- We need to define common values and create the user-friendly language to enhance a sense of community belonging.
- The values need to be clearly defined, which will begin to establish our collective cultural identity.
- We need to communicate these collective values using multimedia, with narratives that inspire thoughts that stir people's emotions, and connect to the creative imagination of the listener.
- We all desire to be recognized and appreciated. The initiative must affirm participation and nurture a sense of ownership.
- We should move towards decentralized government structures, promoting a sense of ownership and nurturing a personal rather than institutional responsibility.

If done effectively, the corporate environment can be the family of the future. We can create a collective identity in our employees or congregation members that reflects the values that are the backbone of our success. The workplace has the potential to be the place where integration is embraced due to the common economic motivation. The collective values of corporations can help to shape the integration strategies of greater society. Business can become one of the key environments of experiential collective truth. The personal experience in this peer group environment creates collective truth and can literally become the place of "belonging." My identity is influenced by the values of my workplace. Now, I will view all aspects of my life from the experiential collective truth of the subculture I belong to. Out in my community, I now represent what we, in our subculture of the workplace, perceive and promote as our values. The marketplace environment can literally be the context for social change.

I believe that we can and should embrace change. We can't embrace change without interaction. We must proactively pursue the engagement of ideals and perspectives. Segregating ourselves to our own familiar surroundings and subcultures won't address the changes coming our way. Historically in any nation, segregation has never been the answer. We must succeed in the integration of the next diverse generation. We are at a point of change, and there is a reason to embrace that change.

The Bible says that life and death are in the power of the tongue. As we face the changes of the near future, we must keep in mind that language is our main currency—we should spend it well!

When communication is the medium, system design and efficiency becomes a key factor in small town mega church success.

Communication systems need to be developed to continually keep all stakeholders informed and engaged. A sense of belonging is created by interactive systems of engagement. The former modern worldview of independent success enhanced isolation rather than interaction. The higher one is on the success ladder, the less contact that person has with the team or customer. In the new atmosphere of social interaction, availability and engagement will not be optional. They will determine the long-term success of the church.

The church is all about relationship. Tasks are not done by lone ranger superstars. Everything we do is done through team interaction. All of our systems and structures require collective input. Personally, I would still be okay with doing things the way we used to do them. I like the minimal red tape and speed of change that a corporate executive team can direct. This may be fast, but it also is the reason why we are not engaging the next generation. They want engagement and involvement in process. Teamwork is almost a natural motivation for the next generation, if the cause is clear. There is a willingness in their generation to have a consensus-driven leadership atmosphere rather than one of a boss to a servant, a teacher to a student, or the lone ranger superstar approach. A consensus-style atmosphere allows for input of all ages and all team members, and this by nature increases one's sense of ownership.

The culture we create will determine the degree of ownership members of the team will experience. If you feel like you have to make all of the decisions, the team will eventually let you. This may build a team of servants, but not self-motivated and self-correcting leadership teams. The leaders we position in the future must have the ability to create interactive cultures; simply managing a department will no longer be sufficient.

We are faced with a fast-paced, ever-changing world. We can no longer build a department and expect it to remain the same for the next twenty years. We need to be innovative as we create relational and clearly defined cultures that will further the cause and identity of the church. An evangelistic movement doesn't just happen; we have to create the culture of evangelism. We also have to create strategies and structures that will allow it to take root and be released. A culture of prayer needs to be created. Anything left to happen on its own will not take root and ultimately have very little impact.

A youth culture is created by music, identity, events, attitudes, facility, and common goals. The youth themselves have created a culture of compassion to meet the needs of those who are oppressed and abused. It isn't enough to just manage a department anymore. We have to provide leadership in a way that creates environments, programs, vision, teams, and communication of progress. A culture of prayer in every department of the church is far better than a prayer meeting in itself. A culture makes the initiative part of who we are, not just what we do. When we are developing our structures and strategies to create cultures or environments rather than programs, we are structuring for long-term success. Our goal needs to be inclusive and engaging to as many people as possible. We start with an equal opportunity to all who express interest. They are free then to rise to leadership as fast as they choose. We call it an open heaven policy. We only limit someone if, during the process, it becomes necessary.

A culture is created by the target age group. We know all people are important, but we have learned by experience that the seventeen to twenty-five-year-olds are the connectors. We have worked with youth for over twenty-five years now, and I have made some observations. We have a mindset in North America towards young people that not only proclaims, but endorses the teenage years as years of trouble. In our words and actions, we show that they are trouble and should be contained or ignored until they come to their senses, usually sometime in their twenties. Our programming and the cultures we created reinforced this thinking.

We have developed a life flow in our church that embraces the seventeen to twenty-five-year-olds. I found that the young teenagers liked my preaching and energy while doing ministry, but I wasn't really their role model. They had their eyes on someone in their late teens or early twenties. Churches build youth departments that appeal to the games-oriented young teenagers and almost force the older teens or young adults to find something else to do. We don't create anything for them, because there aren't enough of them or they don't know what to do with themselves. Well, I know what they can do! They can run the church! They can mentor the next generation and prepare for a great future!

I call them my burning bush generation! I have never seen a generation that has so much talent and creativity. I was travelling with Corey Peebles, a young man in his early twenties, who along with his wife Jeneile are responsible for all of our youth departments. We were going down the road talking about ministry and I could hear a clicking noise as we talked. I finally realized that he was talking to me, enjoying the scenery of the Canadian Rockies, and sending a text message all at the same time! He didn't even have to watch his fingers. I would have to pull over, shut off the radio, and focus on the keypad for ten minutes to send a message as long as the one he sent in about forty-five seconds. I notice it in marketing, TV programming, and many other areas of life. A youth sports show like snowboarding or skateboarding usually has loud music, flashing pictures, and screaming announcers! It gives me a headache. My mind wants to focus on one thought, one scene, or one medium—not all of them at once.

This happens in church as well. My generation is quite content to sit and listen to one medium of presentation. The next generation likes to hear, see, and experience the message in as many mediums as possible all at the same time. We tend to think that it is not possible for us to do this in a small church. However, it is really about the priority you place on making it happen. We can pay off our mortgage and have a facility that is debt-free and full of white hair or we can spend a large portion of our budgets on reaching the next generation in a way that engages their culture.

I started to think about this "on fire" burning bush generation. I wondered why the Lord had given them the ability to process diverse information at such a staggering rate. Why all the multimedia? As I pondered this thought, I believe I received a revelation from the Lord. He has rose up a multimedia generation *because He is a multimedia God!* There is already a generation on the earth today that can outvote the baby boomers. They are children now, but over the next few years they will become the driving force of our governments, faith communities, economy, airwaves, and every other sector of society. This large mass of people will not look to my baby boomer generation for inspiration.

There needs to be someone who can get their attention. I believe the seventeen to twenty-five-year-olds are that generation. They are being prepared by God for Him to move so fast and in so many ways at the same time that if they were not gifted in processing multimedia information, they would miss a large portion of what the Lord is about to do. The next movement won't be about one expression of God like it has been in the past. We have had seasons of evangelists, of prophets, or of successful missions or various outbreaks of expression in the body of Christ. Over time, we have been diverse and have seen and experienced a broad spectrum of God. But the next move will not be about one emphasis; it will be a movement that combines all the expressions and emphases of God at one time. Those who can only see or experience one dimension will miss most of what the Lord desires for us to experience or do. A narrow expression or experience of God will only reach a narrow portion of the next generation. God wants to be God! He is about to express Himself in every way, all at the same time. A multimedia-trained generation will be able to process diverse information at the speed of God!

I believe the seventeen to twenty-five-year-olds of today are gifted with music, media, and passion to get the attention of the next generation—just like in the days of Moses, when his curiosity caused him to approach the burning bush. That's why I call them my burning bush generation! This young multimedia generation that is on fire for God will cause people to come close out of curiosity, and when they do, they will meet with the reality of our God! What a great time to be alive!

We have had some say to us that we can't build a church just for young people. That's not our goal. We have created a life flow for our church *with* our young people, but which includes all ages.

TWELVE

CREATING INTERNAL CULTURES

Momentum and strength is developed by creating the cultures or environments you need to fulfill the vision. If the church has a missions emphasis, you cannot build momentum with only a missions bulletin board or a missions director that makes a presentation one week of the year. You would need to develop a culture of missions through language, message emphasis, atmosphere, programming, conversations, and celebrations.

In a leadership book I read a few years ago, it said "Wanted: Leaders who can create culture; mere managers need not apply!" We are not looking for leaders who can just manage a department, but rather ones who know how to create a culture through the managing, marketing, and mobilization of a vision. The culture you create with your programming, language, and relationship atmosphere can be a powerful force. The culture and atmosphere you create, reflected in the language, flow of services, identity, and emphasis of ministry, are the entities that create a sense of belonging in the members of your church. I have developed a template as a tool to work with to determine and define the life flow and strength of your church.

The Template

Taglines (Defined Vision): The tagline is a reflection or representation of the redemptive purpose or reason that the church exists. You need to take the time to fill in the blanks on the template. Take time thinking through the vision thoroughly enough that you can accurately express it in one short statement.

The tagline defines the vision and gives us a constant reminder of who we are and where we are trying to go. It also reflects our inherent strength.

Goals and Objectives: The next issue on the template are goals or objectives. This statement should reflect the outcome or product produced. In the example, we are using the tagline, "Living in His Presence!" The goal or objective is "Sozo." This is the Greek word translated as "saved" in the New Testament. It means saved, healed, delivered, and made whole! We believe this is the outcome of living in His presence. In our Drayton Valley location, we use "Living Life on Purpose!" as our tagline. This location is focussed on training. The goal then becomes, "Equipping the saints for the work of the ministry." So in one location, the emphasis is on sozo,

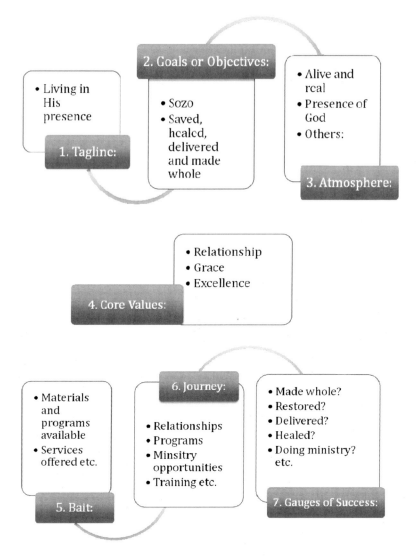

Most of the information in the above template is taken from our Fort Saskatchewan site. The information you use in the seven categories will be unique to your church and vision.

while in the other, it is about equipping for ministry.

Core Values: We should then refer to our core values statement to determine the main "backbone" values that will guide all of our decisions, programs, and emphasis ministries. *There are three main core values at Life Church International,* and out of these core values we can develop some guiding statements:

1. Relationships: Loving God and loving people. Let love inconvenience you.
2. Grace: God's presence and power working in and through you.
3. Excellence: We won't always have the best, but we must do the best with what we have.

Atmosphere (The Pond): The atmosphere we create in the church is very similar at all stages of growth. It is one of the most important factors in our ability to retain visitors. One of our youth pastors came up with the term "effective relational engagement." I like this thought, because people will make a decision about how they feel about a church within minutes of walking through the doors. If the people are busy visiting with each other and pay little or no attention to incoming visitors, we are sending a message about who we are and how much we value them. On the other hand, if people are greeted at the door with a friendly hello, given some information about the service, introduced to the pastors, youth leaders, or children workers, and shown parts of the facility (if time allows), then we have just improved the odds of them returning.

I was at a large conference in Australia a couple of years ago and the customer service I experienced there was incredible. I watched as a team of hundreds of workers cared for the thousands of guests who attended the conference. I was very impressed. I thought I would put the team to the test on the Sunday night service back at the church. I walked from my hotel to the church dressed casually so I didn't draw any unusual attention. As soon as I set foot on the parking lot of the church, I was greeted by a young man with a warm, "Good evening, sir! Are you here for the evening service?" When I indicated that I was, he directed me across the parking lot to the big double doors where he said there would be ushers to direct me from there. At the doors, I was warmly greeted, given info about the church, and directed to the sanctuary doors. It was at the doors of the sanctuary that I was asked more questions. Here, the usher discovered that I was a pastor who was attending their conference and he directed me to my seat. Wow! I was feeling so special… I think I could have just went home right then and felt I had been blessed! This is the power of atmosphere. It says something about who you are and what is important to you. They said I was important to them and it proved to be more than just words; they treated me like I was, too.

The atmosphere you create must be compatible with the people you are trying to engage. The challenge of a small town church is the same challenge that medical doctors encounter in their practices. A doctor who lives in a major population base can specialize as an eye doctor and still have enough patients to sustain his or her business. An eye doctor in a small town will not have the customer base needed to sustain his practice, however, so he must diversify in the services he offers. The smaller the community, the broader the services offered. The same principle applies to the church. We cannot build a church with a specialty ministry that connects with only a few. We must create an atmosphere and flow that reflects our identity and calling, but not in a way that repels others who may not fit the age or image we are targeting.

Another factor to keep in mind is that most of the workers available to help you in the design or cleanliness of the church are women. With this in mind, we need to be careful that our atmosphere doesn't become so feminine and flowery that it makes men uncomfortable. Many times, I think we have trouble getting men involved in church because they see it as feminine and emotional. Try to keep some balance so that the men can feel like they belong, too! I may not hang deer heads on the door, but who knows?

We use music before and after the service to help create a lively atmosphere to encourage fun and fellowship. We even started a coffee bar to open after the services so that people can hang around and visit if they like. The goal is to have a fun-filled, high-energy environment. I hate funeral home music in the background when I am trying to just have some fun with my friends. Make it alive!

The atmosphere we create can make or break a church. Over time, it will be developed either by design or by default. We need to be intentional about the atmosphere we create. A positive atmosphere will build relationships, stir the vision, provide a sense of belonging, and even facilitate some networking for business ventures. It can be one of the greatest keys to building a strong relationship-based church. I see it as a fisherman sees a pond; it is the gathering place of the fish, but now we have to catch them!

The Bait (What's in it for me?): Everyone goes to church for a reason. It may be that they were raised going to church or that they are seeking friendship, purpose, opportunity, training—or, who knows, even God! Of course, I am being sarcastic, but my point is that everyone is looking for something. The atmosphere you create is like a pond to a fisherman, but anyone who has tried fishing knows that although the fish may be there, if you are not using the right bait you still won't catch them.

I understand that the main factor in a church should be the inherent sense of the presence of God, but beyond the initial meeting with God, people have many things they look for in a church. They may be looking for programs for their teens or kids, or maybe training for themselves. They may have a special interest in missions or a heart for meeting the needs of the city. The list of possible interests would be endless. This is why we need to determine who we are, what we are called to do, and who are we trying to reach. Everyone is welcome, but all churches have a unique nature and natural strength. The bait is cast out by personal contact with people, the language we use, the signage we put on the walls, the programs we promote, and the materials we place in visitors' hands.

The bait needs to be in harmony with the natural strength and purpose of the church. If we put out information giving an impression of what our church is all about, but in reality we put very little effort in that direction—or don't really have a natural ability to succeed in that area—people will very quickly see the weakness and wander away. The goal is to be true to your calling and be real about where you are at in the journey.

The bait needs to be a promotion of what you can offer in your journey. It may be leadership development, missions, music program, youth, kids, or any other strength you may have. The clearer you are in communicating your core strengths, the better the chances of catching the attention and interest of those who visit. We are always quick to promote our youth program, our music, and the fact that we are just real people. Beyond these basic qualities that are common to all of our locations, we work hard to identify and promote the core strengths of each location. We offer leadership training, ministry development, and are in the process of developing prayer rooms and special small group gatherings to accommodate site-specific visions.

The bait is also delivered in the messages preached. You get what you preach. If you desire to reach teens, but preach to the elderly, you will get what you preach, not what you want. If you are not attracting or keeping the kind of people you think you are called to reach, I would encourage you to check your bait!

The Journey: The journey is the process of getting from vision to reality. The journey needs to reflect the process and programming you use. It is the life flow of the church. This is an important part of the template to think through. All programming at every age and every department must feed the vision and goals of the church. Programs without vision will give you a sense of movement without a destination. On the other hand, a destination without the proper programming will sound exciting, but will always be out there somewhere out of reach of your present reality. Programming feeds the success of the vision. Think through your vision and the limitations or opportunities that you or others following you will encounter along the way. Each one of these limitations or opportunities are keys to the development of programming that aligns with the vision and helps to guide the congregation members in a common direction towards a specific goal.

At this stage, I want to encourage you to stay focussed. There are many good things you could do, and will be presented to you as things people think you should do, but don't get distracted. Stay true to your calling. When you have enough core strength and momentum established in your vision, you can take a look at some other ministry opportunities, but at this stage they are distractions.

You will find that as you define your calling and develop programming to lead you in a common direction, there will be cliques that start to form in the church. Most churches tend to fight against cliques, but I think they are good as long as everyone is a part of one. We try to identify the reason for each clique or their special interest, and then send new people that way if they appear to have the same nature. If new people can find a task-oriented or special interest fellowship group, they will quickly feel like they belong. The journey needs to have both large group and small group social dynamics. This gives everyone a sense of being a part of something big while at the same time building personal relationships in a small group.

Our programming needs to be both effective and efficient. Sometimes we have efficient programs that have reporting systems complete with strategies and structures, where everyone knows their roles and responsibilities, but doesn't produce anything. We can also have effective ministry happening that is poorly administered, so the effectiveness is reduced by a lack of efficiency. We need to strive for effective and efficient programming if we are going to lead large groups of people to any definable destination. While determining the programming for the journey, use the bookends model. The terminology during the brainstorming sessions should not only be about the journey *from* something, but also have a strong emphasis on running *to* something, such as "Out of a victim mentality, running *to* victorious living," or "Out from a poverty mindset, running *to* an abundant life."

It is important to develop a system that allows each church member to track his or her own progress. Anything that cannot be measured cannot be sustained. Our Drayton Valley location has modified a passport concept that we adopted from another church. The pages of the passport identifies each of the training programs we offer, and as the individual completes each program he or she gets a signature of completion from the instructor or department head on that page of their passport. On completion of all the ministries of the passport, they can apply for a recognition of ministry certificate and progress on to other levels of recognition, up to and including being ordained by LCI. The programming of the journey needs to have continuity for all departments and all ages. Remember, all programming must feed the success of and strengthen the corporate vision!

There are two perspectives to think about while building a church of any size. Are you building a cruise ship or a battle ship? Are you building a hospital or an embassy? Of course, the proper answer is both. An overemphasis of either extreme can limit the efficiency or effectiveness of the church. A church that has a hospital mentality in their journey will address the sick, but never make them ambassadors for the King. If we overemphasise an embassy environment, those who are not feeling strong or need some care will not feel like they fit in. I recently coined the phrase, "We are always at war, but not always in battle!" This reflects the reality that there is an ongoing war to win, but we are not always fighting; sometimes we need to do a victory celebration along the way!

Gauges of Success (Mature and Complete, Lacking Noth-

ing): This is a very important principle to think through. We tend to gauge success only by numbers, but if that is the only gauge the kingdom has ever used, then the Apostle Paul or Jesus Himself would be considered failures in their ministry. Numbers are important, but they are not the only gauge of our success. Jesus changed the world forever with only a handful of people. The Apostle Paul found himself alone during his final days of imprisonment in Rome. We can also get so focussed on where we are going that we never stop to think about what it looks like if we ever arrive. The Christian journey doesn't really lead us to a destination, but rather on a continuous process of discovery for ourselves, during which we are constantly helping others. We need to be able to identify when we have achieved any level of success on the way. The gauges of success we use should confirm our calling. If training leaders was our intent, then a good gauge would be seen in how many leaders we have established. In the case of our sozo vision, we have identified that, to us, sozo is more than just physical healing—it can be measured in the healing of relationships, the restoration of ministries, the healing of wounded Christians, or deliverance from addictions. Our programming facilitates the journey, and our gauges of success confirms our calling. Our gauges of success need to be custom-designed to match the vision, goals, and journey of the church. They provide us measuring tools that are not based on comparisons to the church down the street.

The best way to ensure that we keep moving forward is to stop and celebrate the successes we have achieved along the way. Once we have celebrated an accomplishment, it is very unlikely that we will ever revert backwards from that point. Celebration is the greatest safeguard against backsliding.

Gauges of success can be described and defined in so many ways. They can include academic achievements, ministry experience, life skill development, character, excellence, networking, responsible lifestyles, and purpose, among others. It really isn't important what the gauge is, as long as it truly reflects the vision, goals, and objectives of the church and can be used as a marker for achievement on the journey. Gauges should complete the cycle from visiting, joining, engaging, and eventually becoming a leader that helps others in their journey to maturity.

If you will take the time to work through the template, you will find that you have just defined your calling, set your goals, identified key strengths, developed your strategies, and established a gauge to monitor your success.

THIRTEEN

BREAKING THE CYCLES OF AVERAGE

One of the greatest enemies of the North American church is the acceptance of the idea that settling for average is good enough. Some of us even strive to be a little above average, but we lose ambition as soon as we feel we have reached that goal. There are so many factors in breaking the cycles of average that could be addressed that it could easily fill another book all on its own. There are so many pressures to align with the status quo, but status quo is only a fancy word for average!

When you consider church history, you start to see that the Lord breaks out beyond the familiar and starts to do things that seem strange at the time. Due to unfamiliar expressions or manifestations, we start to feel uncomfortable and even threatened. In defence of what we think is normal, we start to put pressure on the new to conform to the familiar, or the status quo. By doing so, we eventually journey back to average. This breaking out and reverting back creates a cycle that eventually leads us right back to where we began. I see it in generations. One generation works hard to break away from the traditions of their fathers only to find years down the road that they have become just like them. The cycle is subtle yet continual. One day and one decision at a time, we break out and then start to revert back to average.

To break out of the cycles of average, we have to first decide that status quo is not where we want to be. By this, we are saying that we will be different. There will be those who don't like what we are doing. There will be those who will not come to the church because we are not like everybody else. Many will leave one church because they don't feel they are being fed, or don't like the flow of the services, only to arrive at another church and try to get them to conform to the ways of the church they just left. I am not looking to be conformed; I want to be transformed. A transformation isn't about a subtle change or a season of time in my life. It is about the old man dying and the new man coming alive. In order to break the cycles of average, we must be willing to let the old die! I would even say it stronger: we must be willing to kill the old in order to embrace the new. When you break out, don't go back. When you break out, stay out!

In order to break out in the first place, you need to be aware of your breakthrough anointing. We all have one. King David had a breakthrough anointing in worship. As he worshiped, a distressing spirit would lift. Abraham had an anointing of faith. Paul had one of wisdom. Everyone has one, and so does every church. Pay attention to what breaks you out, embrace it, and don't go back. Change whatever needs to be changed in order to accommodate the breakout that will keep you out! Focus on it in every way, because what you focus on will expand.

Developing a sense of urgency will help you to break the cycle of average. Most of our programming or outreaches tend to have unlimited timeframes. We approach soul winning, or change of any kind for that matter, as something we can do over a long period of time. But what about today? Right now? Why do we make plans that we will only carry out some time in the future when we could be making a plan and taking the first step right now? The body of Christ has mastered the art of procrastination. We are stuck in a mindset that says, "Process is sufficient, results are optional."

We all have a good deed or a good idea about what we will do someday instead of today. We have a neighbour we will witness to sometime, but not at this time. We make all kinds of spiritual excuses, but in reality it is really an issue of procrastination. The real problem is that we have all fallen into the pattern, so we think procrastination is normal. We all need to ask the Lord to give us a sense of urgency. There may not be another time. Our neighbour may move or die, or we may not be here to get another chance. We all believe that the Lord is returning someday, but we live like we don't really believe it will be this day, or one in the foreseeable future.

Negativity is also considered to be normal and it will keep you conforming to average. Anytime you try to break out of anything, you will be assaulted with criticism from the status quo or the average. It is made to sound spiritual, so we respond to it like it was a word from God Himself. This strategy of the devil goes all the way back to the Garden of Eden. He lied about God's motives and of-fered something to Adam and Eve that they already had in fullness with God. He got them into fellowship with his negativity and by doing so caused them to be positioned in disobedience to what the Lord had told them. God instructed them not to eat from the tree of the knowledge of good and evil. The devil got them to come close to it and have discussion with him about the motives and na-ture of God. As soon as they ate from the tree of knowledge of good and evil, they stepped into disobedience with God. This is hard to break out of, because we are positioned in disobedience. God told them to eat from the tree of life. They were positioned at the tree of knowledge of good and evil. The disobedience sepa-rated them from the power and authority of God. That is why it is so hard to break out.

When we get caught in it, we find ourselves running around trying to put out the fires of offence and strife. We pray, but don't break out; we work harder, only to get worn out. It has us trapped in a continual battle we can't win.

At this time, we have two choices. One, we could conform to the pressures, adjust back to the status quo, and accept life as it always has been; or two, we could do what the Lord has been tell-ing us to do in the first place: "Eat off the other tree!" This means simply, but unwaveringly, moving away from the discussion and from those who try to draw you in, and moving towards life. Eat from the tree that brings life. That tree will silence the negativity and break you out of the cycle of average!

Wallowing in mediocrity becomes the comfort zone of our life, and it is hard to break free. There are so many areas of our lives that need to be adjusted to truly change. This causes us to get so overwhelmed that we tend to surrender to our perspective of what we consider average, or perhaps slightly above at best. We can't change everything in one day, but everything we change today moves us one step closer to victory. I like to say, "Today is the first day of the rest of your life!" After all, it is… and we should make it count.

I like to break things down as I am planning anything. When I am contemplating change, I like to list all the things I can think of that needs to be changed in order for me to reach my goals. If the list has twelve items identified, I then start to prioritize the top six. From the top six, I choose the top three, and from the top three, I choose the number one issue to be addressed for me to move forward. Then I take action on that one step immediately. As I get victory over the first issue, I move on to the next one on my list.

I once read somewhere about a Principle of Five. If you had a large tree in your yard that you wished to cut down, but you only had a small axe to work with, if you took that small axe and everyday went up to the tree and struck it five times, eventually that tree would fall! Change comes slow, but even continual slow change over a period of time can cause big change to take place. Give yourself credit for every small change you make and one step at a time break out of the cycle of average.

The same principles that apply to the individual apply to the church. We need to know what our breakthrough anointing is, kill some programming, and then change one thing at a time… or make many small changes to create a big change. There are always those who resist change, and if you submit your time and emotions to them, they will force you back to average. I honour these types of people and respect their views, but I will not give them a lot of my time or let them influence my thinking. I will intentionally hang around with those who are embracing change, those who have positive suggestions and bring credible options to the table.

Most of the time, people resist change due to past experiences that caused them pain. Many times, we don't even realize we are doing it. We can't even identify the source when we stop to think about it. This is because it is something that we may have forgotten in our mind, but our emotions carry the memory. We may not know why we feel the way we do, but we certainly are aware of the feeling. A lot of fear of change is due to past attempts at change that didn't work out so well. It caused some relational or emotional pain that cause us to subconsciously resist going back there. As soon as we start to break out, the old internal warning bell goes off to remind us of the pain we went through in the past, and we fight to avoid the pain by embracing the status quo.

In order to deal with this inner resistance to change while moving your church or department out of average, you have to clearly define what changes are in store and why they are necessary. People will not feel comfortable with the change until they find their role and develop and feel confident with their new skills. There is great fear in many that if we break away from average, they may not be able to have the same position or influence they now enjoy. So again, many small changes can create big change. Break it down. Address the most important issues first, and then step by step move away from average.

Above all, we have to learn to live and do ministry beyond discouragement. I think this is one of the greatest barriers to breaking out of average. When we try so hard and so many things need to change in order to break out and stay out, we can fall into discouragement… and discouragement will return you to average. It is human nature to make decisions with our emotions and then try to justify them with logic. Knowing this, we should do what is logical, wise, and right to break out, and then keep doing it until our emotions adjust. The paradigms of our past determine the perspectives of the present, but we can shift the paradigm of the present to create a new future!

One of the best tools for breakout is to make change fun. Use multimedia presentations, if you can, to promote your objectives in a way that looks like fun. Visual presentations have much more impact than an announcement on its own. You will never think of every variation or obstacle that will present itself during seasons of change, though, so don't get caught up in too much detail. Plan what you can and then release it, weed it as you go, and then align it to the greater vision as it starts to mature. It is much easier to have a discussion about an initiative's effectiveness if it has matured to the point of being able to see it work. As long as you know enough about the goal before you start, enough to be sure that it is the right direction, you can launch it, weed it out, and align it as you go.

FOURTEEN

BUILDING MOMENTUM

I f you will take the time the fill in the blanks of the template, you will be able to define your vision, clarify your goals and objectives, determine your core values, create the atmospheres, establish your programming for the journey, and identify your gauges of success. Now we can focus on the speed of growth by creating momentum.

Momentum is not an event, nor is it a measurement of one particular season. Momentum comes from a series of events and seasons that build one upon the other. It is created by all departments and all ages being actively engaged and feeding into the vision. It is something that is measurable and sustainable. We build and maintain momentum.

Momentum starts with having an understanding of the natural

rhythms of your region. In an agricultural area, we certainly don't want to have a conference during harvest season, since nobody will be available. In Canada, we have natural weather seasons to deal with. In the winter months, people tend to be available and interested in training seminars or conferences. During our short summer season, we all take holidays to enjoy some sunshine. The dynamics of the church changes quite a bit from May's long weekend through Labour Day. Leading up to this summer season, we run all programs for all ages. During the summer months, many churches shut down their programs rather than replace them with something that matches the season. We don't shut down all the programs, but we do modify their function and focus.

I compare it to ocean winds that drive a sailing ship. When the wind dies down, there is still momentum created by the current of the water. The ship's speed may have changed, but there is still movement. The entity creating the movement has changed, but the ship is still able to press on to its destination.

What we determined from this picture was that during the summer months, when the strength of our programming dies down, we can still move forward if we tap into a different way of doing church. We started "Fun in the Son," an initiative that all departments work on. Each department hosts BBQs or fun events to gather those who are available. We don't run our life houses in the summer months, but we do have life house group events. We do things for all departments and all ages throughout the summer, like an annual river raft and BBQ, golf games, picnics, fishing derby, and lots of backyard or campground fire pit visiting. These fun events not only keep the church connected, but create an environment to meet new people.

We have found over the past seven years of summer strategies that this has become our best church growth season of the year. It keeps people connected, gathers new members, and creates momentum for the fall season. When the fall programming kicks in, it is like the wind hitting our sails, but since we are already in motion, we pick up speed quickly. You need to identify and be in harmony with your regional rhythms in order to maintain momentum.

Another key to momentum building comes with your selection and preparation of special guests and speakers. I see many small churches invite anyone who has a unique or powerful ministry to the church. This sounds like a great idea, and is even very entertaining for the saints, but it may not grow a church. In fact, it can totally backfire and cause church members to see their pastors as less able or equipped than the church's guest speakers have been. To build momentum with guest ministries, we first need to choose the guests wisely by knowing where we are trying to go, what emphasis of ministry are trying to deposit in the church, and what attitudes will be developed by this guest. If we think these things through and it is determined that the guest in question is the right match for the season of time we are in, we can start the process.

We don't just have a guest and hope they do all that needs to be done. We ramp up to the guest's visit. We start in advance, building momentum and getting everyone possible focussed on the core message and purpose for the visit. During the visit of the guest ministry, they do all the work, and if we have prepared properly, it should be a dynamic time. The real test of the leadership and skill of the pastor comes into play the week after the guest leaves. It is like a relay race. If the pastor stands up the next week and goes a different direction or drops the baton in any way, they have just shot themselves in the foot. The people will see what appears to be a lower level ministry and start to respond to him or her at that lower level. They then start to have conversations about the good old days when this guest came or that guest came and sit neutral, waiting for another guest to come and inspire them again, rather than talking about what happened in the church that Sunday and being unable to wait for the next Sunday to come!

I also like to ride the horse that's running! We build fluid leadership teams so that we can make adjustments quickly. Sometimes in our search for the fastest horse, we make too many changes... but in general it works pretty well. We look for what is stirring, and in what age group, and try to embrace it as quickly as possible. We also need to recognize when the horse has stopped and be brave enough to get off and move on to what the Lord does next.

Our messages make a great impact on our momentum. Due to the fact that we have many preachers, we try to identify themes for seasons of time. It isn't systematic so much as it is inspirational. We grab hold of a God thought that seems to inspire us for that season of time. The best preaching is done by preaching that which stirs you; if you aren't stirred about the message, it won't inspire anyone else either! I then encourage all of our preachers to listen to their own messages. While listening to yourself, pretend you are someone else hearing this message for the first time. Would you want to listen again? Where you inspired? Confused? Troubled? Do you now have more questions than answers? Was it relevant to your life, or was it just information that's not really usable? When I listen to one of my messages, I break it down into a beginning, middle, and end, and then measure momentum of the message, clarity of the key points, crowd response, and body language. If it's a video recording, I can also take into account tone and general impact. I make a list of what I am going to critique myself with and I score each item from one to ten. If you try this technique, attempt to stay in the middle of criticism. Don't be too hard on yourself. This is a learning tool and a life journey, but don't let yourself off the hook with excuses either.

While studying about the exodus from Egypt, I noticed a pattern for initiating and maintaining momentum. While still in captivity, God shared a vision. He told the Israelites about a land flowing with milk and honey. He gave them a clear picture of future possibilities. This vision of a better place was enough to get the people mobilized, but eventually Joshua and Caleb had to display the fruit they had brought back from the promised land in order to inspire some to keep going forward. I thought, "Cast the vision—display the fruit!" This is a key to momentum. We can get people moving in a direction with vision alone for a season of time, but eventually if they don't see any fruit, they will turn in another direction or get discouraged along the way.

One of the greatest strengths of a revival is that people continually display what God is doing in their lives. While working through the process of the template, you can clearly declare the vision and goals and how the journey is going to take place. But as soon as possible, we need to display the fruit by showing how the vision is benefiting people's lives. The fruit needs to be relevant to the vision and goals. A church with an emphasis on leadership development should have some public recognition and celebration services to display the fruit of those who have achieved milestones along the way. If evangelism is the main focus, then display the souls saved and so on.

A common error, especially in a small church where there are a limited number of leaders, is to build programs that you think you need, and then try to get leaders to run them and God to fill them. Sometimes the people involved are miserable, because it is not something they enjoy or desire to do. There are some key departments at every level, even in the early days of start-up, but beyond the basics of church, we should do all we can to build around the leaders, people, and giftings that God has sent us. As we succeed in matching giftings and need, we have just released someone into their passion and calling and strengthened the local church with a self-motivated team.

I have already stated that events don't necessarily grow churches, but they can create or enhance momentum if the right event is executed the right way. A successful event can attract new interest, but we must use effective relational engagement and follow-up after the event or the church will not grow. I have heard that if you can get someone into your church for any reason, it increases the odds of them joining by eighty percent. I believe, however that though it may increase the odds, it doesn't get the job done unless you are effective in follow-up. This is one reason why I am not really a big fan of a lot of inter-church events. We can't follow-up with someone who is already part of another church. I know there are other reasons to get together as one body, but my point is that we can spend so much time and energy on inter-church events that we never get around to building our own church. I think the best form of advertising is found in the ability to get your own people talking about the church in a positive and exciting way. This creates a buzz in the congregation. It may be about the music program, youth movement, church growth, souls saved, or ministry accomplished.

Many churches have exploded in growth due to strange manifestations and unexplainable events. We have all read the books or heard of things like a pulpit breaking in two during a preacher's message, gold dust falling from thin air, angels appearing in services, or people simply rolling on the floor as they are overcome by the presence of God. This may happen from time to time, but it shouldn't be one of your main goals. I want people to be excited about a real God with real people! I want to hear of life-changing testimonies that inspire others to see church as a place to find help and strength and a place to meet with our God.

One of the strangest things about church growth comes in the form of what might seem like an oxymoron: If we get too focussed on growth, the church will not grow! The goal is to grow the church, but the way we try to do it sometimes becomes self-defeating. We try to gather lots of people. Sounds good, right? But gathering lots of people take lots of time, and if we don't have leaders and teams in place, we won't be able to get to everyone fast enough to engage them or meet their needs, answer their questions, or deal with their concerns. As a result, the church continues to gather people in the front door, but loses them out the back.

Church needs to be about relationship and care. We need to spend as much time (or more) on strengthening the core of the people we have as we do gathering new ones. Many times, we are so focussed at going fishing that we miss the fish that have jumped into our boat! I keep my eyes on both the core and the total number of people attending.

An overemphasized initiative on strengthening the core without adding new people will build a deeper life club that eventually becomes stale and bitter! It is never too soon to train leaders or build and resource our teams. We are constantly working on more efficient ways to train and resource our people. We have an attitude of bigness because big people build big churches. We produce as many products as we can that can resource our teams. Like this book on church growth, for example. We also use teaching CDs, training seminars, and one-on-one mentoring. Many times, a small church will think there is not a need for more leaders, so they don't put any time or resources into creating them. The Lord will never fill a need that you don't even believe is there. I always want more leaders! As the leaders rise up or come and join us, we instantly expand our capacity to influence our communities on another level. This creates the need and opportunity for more leaders.

The point is this, produce products, gather resources, and take the time to train your leaders. In turn, they will maintain your momentum. Becoming a good leader often means that you have to become a good reader. I have heard it said many times, "Leaders are readers." This simply means that we need to be constantly feeding our minds. There is so much to learn, so we are always watching for books or resource materials for our leaders.

We should never stop learning and growing. We believe that every pastor should have a pastor or mentor that they can turn to. There are a lot of pastors trying to connect to someone who can be there for them, but they don't know how to choose whom to connect with. I was recently at a church leadership training seminar and heard three keys for a pastor to finding the right pastor or mentor for themselves.

1. They must love you.

2. They must believe in you and your vision.
3. They must be able to lift you up to another level.

I like these guidelines and have applied them to my life and ministry. I also set them as guidelines for myself when others ask me to be their pastor. Do I love them? Do I believe in them and their calling? Can I lift them up to another level? If you are reading this book and you are looking for a pastor, give us a call. We may be a match! No matter what level of leader you are mentoring, it is a good idea to spend time and resources on their success. We should intentionally expose them to greatness in the direction they want to grow in.

Keep in mind that we need to display the fruit as we celebrate each team or individual success. Recently we had one of our faithful young worship leaders go to Nashville to record an album. What a great opportunity this was to celebrate the fruit of a church that says we are spiritual mothers and fathers raising up sons and daughters to go higher and further than we ever did. I've never gone to record in Nashville—yet!—but I can sure celebrate one of our sons that did. It means we both succeeded! A celebration will always add to momentum.

Momentum is created by environments, so if we want to have leaders, we have to create environments for leaders, and so on. There comes a time when the pastor has to take his or her hands off every initiative and give it a sail or fail test. If the program will only run if you have your hands on it, then it will eventually kill your ability to expand your ministry. Therefore, it will limit your potential. Give it a push, let it go, and see how it sails. If you have spent the time mentoring the team, it should go some distance before you need to step in and give it another push!

There are times when we find ourselves in what some military people call a kill zone. This is when the enemy ambushes your team and has you trapped. The enemy's goal isn't to try to hit you, but to get you to shoot back until you use up all of your ammunition; then they can just walk in and kill you. The only response to finding yourself in a kill zone is to go forward no matter what! There are times when we have to rise up and lead the church forward no matter how many bullets are flying, how many troops have disserted, or how unlikely our survival may be. The outcome of a brave and bold response is hard to predict, but not being brave and bold has a very definable and predictable end to it.

While creating and maintaining momentum, keep your eyes on the growth plateaus and make leadership and team changes before you arrive at them. A lack of change will slow or stall your momentum. We also need to understand the threshold signs of church growth. There are points where our leaders and teams have reached maximum capacity for their experience and knowledge. There are many signs of this, like frustrations, offences, leaders quitting, and losing people. If you pay attention to yourself and your team, you will quickly start to recognize the changes in attitudes or relationships. Each church needs to identify and understand the expressions of their threshold. When you are nearing a growth threshold, it is very important to focus on the next level of leadership training. If you can get enough core leaders to the next level before the demand becomes too high, you will transition without too many problems.

We also need to recognize when we have hit critical mass in our community influence. Now is the time to take the mayor for lunch to offer help and support. If done while you have twenty people in your church in a town or city of ten thousand or more, he may appreciate the intent, but know you are limited in what you can do for him beyond prayer. A church of five hundred in the same town will get much more attention. Don't try to use it too soon, but don't miss it when it comes!

Another strange principle in church growth is to let people leave if they want to leave. We will follow up on someone who has not been around for a while, but if we know they want to leave for whatever reason, we let them go. We have found that trying to convince someone who is unhappy to stay only gives them more time to build relationships and take more people with them when they eventually leave. We can kill momentum by dragging on some of these relational issues, in the vain hopes of winning them over. Get it over with quickly. Address what you can, deal with your emotions, and start going forward.

There was a hit song many years ago on the radio that said, "Going to get along without you now / Got along without you before I met you / Going to get along without you now." I use this song in my head to help get past the difficult emotions of people deciding they don't like our vision or have left for some reason beyond our control.

As stated earlier, in real estate the key is location, location, location… but in church, it's vision, vision, vision. We need to develop our vision in a way that is simple and accurate so that everyone can use it. The simpler and clearer the vision, the more it will be declared, and the more it's declared, the more impact it will have. We need to market who we are and what we are called to do. The marketing needs to be done internally in the church, and externally in the city. The city will think about the church what you teach them to think about the church. If you leave an image void, it will get filled, but not necessarily with the truth you desire to be known for. Your credibility should be guarded. It takes years to build credibility, but only minutes to lose it. Vision and credibility are day-by-day tasks. Build them one day at a time and every day of the week, here a little and there a little, precept upon precept, line upon line. The goal is to effectively serve the redemptive purpose of the city and effectively take your place in the part that your church plays in pastoring your community.

A vision and an image take years to build, so it is important for us to buy into the long-term vision for our city. We may not all be in one location for the rest of our lives, but we should build our vision as though we are going to be. We try to work out a three-year plan with a twenty-year intent. Momentum is built or reduced every time we get together. Every service, every event, and every meeting matters. There aren't any days that don't matter, or people who don't matter, or services that don't matter. Every one of them has an effect on our momentum. We need to make every day, every relationship, and every event count.

FIFTEEN

MOBILIZING MARKETPLACE MINISTRIES

The business owners group vision statement is as follows:

To create a collective strength or synergy by the integration of the local church, intercessory prayer, and marketplace ministries. This synergy will create wealth, promote Christian values, and take social and economical responsibility for the well-being of our city and nation.

The business owners group has four basic core functions. The first and most obvious, of course, is to create wealth for the Kingdom. I believe that there are marketplace leaders who have a specific calling to do business and create wealth. We have so many bad opinions of wealth and those who are called and gifted to create it. Even in Hollywood, the villain is usually a very successful business leader who went bad and now is a threat to mankind. The reality is that many humane and honourable initiatives are built and maintained by wealthy people with compassionate hearts.

During the development of our marketplace business owners group, we had many discussions about calling business leaders "ministers." This term has been reserved for the clergy. The body of Christ has reduced most of what happens in ministry down to the role and responsibility of the clergy, while the scripture clearly states—in Ephesians 4, for example—that the role of the clergy is to equip the saints for the work of the ministry. I think we get caught up on a lot of terminology when we really don't need to.

I believe it is an issue of time versus tasks. The debate seemed to focus around the issue that a clergy minister is more able to connect with God or had a closer position with God than a marketplace minister can have. I think this paradigm of thinking is what causes the problem in itself. It isn't an issue of closeness to God; it is an issue of time versus tasks. The foundational requirement of both roles are exactly the same. Integrity, purity, character, faith, prayer, fellowship, honour, accountability, servanthood, and all the other qualities we could add to the list. As we start to describe the main role or functions of the two, we start to see a lot of difference. A clergy minister spends a lot of time with visitations, weddings, care for the needy, counselling, preaching, and teaching Bible doctrines. A business leader spends much of his or her time with sales and marketing, strategy meetings, and customer service. This doesn't mean that a business leader cannot take time to minister as a clergy minister would, or that a pastor wouldn't spend any time on the business of church. To me, it is an issue of time versus tasks. If clergy ministers spent all of their time doing business, then the care of the people would not be taking place and they would no longer be identified as clergy ministers. Likewise, if business leaders spent all of their time meeting with and counselling people, they wouldn't build a successful company and would no longer be considered business leaders at all. What I have proposed is that we need a crosspollination of both groups. The clergy desperately needs the wisdom of successful business leaders. There are so many financial issues that arise in the business of church that most pastors are ill-equipped to deal with.

If I could put this scenario into another environment for a moment, I think it will reinforce my logic in this. We tend to try to change foreign cultures by planting churches and building orphanages. There is nothing wrong with doing either of these things, but it hasn't really resolved the problem of systemic poverty. I believe we should work through business and enterprise to enable people to become self-sufficient. If we started a business with Christian values and, through relationship with our employees, we had an opportunity to share the gospel, we would be meeting both their natural and spiritual needs. A business leader who starts a company based on Christian values can reach his or her employees through daily interaction.

At some point, however, a time versus task issue will arise. If they continue to spend their time ministering to their employees, they won't have time to build the company. The employees all have families and meeting their needs takes a lot of time. Many companies have hired a company chaplain to spend time meeting with and counselling employees. If a company or outreach reaches a certain level of effectiveness, it becomes impossible for the chaplain to meet with each family individually for every issue. It therefore becomes logical to gather them on a regular basis to talk with them as a group. We have just launched a church!

I believe the crosspollination of business leaders and clergy is a good goal. Business leaders can develop more ministry skills and the clergy can develop a greater wisdom for the business of church. Both are needed in the Kingdom and should honour the special contribution each will make.

The second function or responsibility of the business owners group is in their ability to be the gatekeepers of the community. Our marketplace leaders have far more influence to shape the present or future state of our cities than the ministerial leaders do. Their voice is heard by community leaders and politicians. This is why I call them gatekeepers. A united business owners group has the influence and responsibility to open or close the gate of our city, and in the process shape the future well-being of the community. During my years as a politician, I experienced firsthand the power of the marketplace to shape a city, and I know that business leaders can and should be the strongest lobbying group. Their voice is heard and does make a difference. The church has mass numbers that politicians may court in an election year, but they need the favour and support of the marketplace leaders every year if they want to get anything done.

The third function of a marketplace ministry is to shoulder the vision of the local church. This by nature means that the local church has identified the reason that the Lord brought them together in that particular city in the first place. I am not suggesting that a marketplace leader has an obligation to shoulder every idea or whim of a pastor; I am talking about shouldering the long-term vision of the local church. The reality is that the local church is the equipping centre that facilitates the work of God in the city, but the actual work happens beyond the four walls of the building—out in the marketplace! So the clergy is actually working towards and helping to facilitate the success of those who do ministry beyond the four walls of the church. When this partnership is in place, marketplace leaders should take ownership of and shoulder or carry the vision.

The last core function of the marketplace group is to develop the blueprint of city transformation. We have heard many messages and read many books about city transformation over the last number of years, but it tends to remain theoretical, not functioning reality! I think one of the main reasons for this is that the clergy tends to be the ones coming up with the strategies and hoping that marketplace leaders will get it done. I believe we would have a much stronger initiative when the marketplace leaders develop a Christian influence blueprint for every sector of our society. They have the insight and experience to know what the needs are, what is driving the economy, who we need to influence, and how to get things done. A marketplace group can raise more capital for the kingdom in one meeting than six months of special offerings in the local church.

We teach the five-fold governing ministries of apostle, prophet, evangelist, pastor, and teacher. I think, however, that there is one not stated, but seen by example... Jesus, the CEO! We need them all! I believe the marketplace is the battleground for our cities and nations. The more we partner the church and marketplace strengths, the greater the impact and success we will both have.

There are three levels and expressions in the business owners group.

The first is to use and promote Christian values in the city. This includes reaching people with the Gospel and gathering together for worship. It also involves running prayer meetings, home groups, or Bible studies for employees or others that they may engage in the process of doing business.

The second level is for those who wish to do more by joining a lobbying group that interacts with the political process, to engage other business leaders and politicians or educators addressing community issues, to help start or grow businesses God's way, to mentor leaders, and to raise funds for the vision. In short, to build the kingdom.

The third level is to engage the big picture of national or international issues, and to join in the spiritual warfare prayer ministry. This involves helping to expand the ministry to other cities, plant more churches, build training centres, or start new businesses in foreign lands. It also should incorporate partnering with the church's organizational leaders in strategy meetings or to stand strong during seasons of battle. This partnership includes the care of the pastors to ensure their present and future well-being.

I have launched Gary Carter Ministries to facilitate this relationship. The goal of this level of commitment is to enable me and our team to get where we need to go, buy what we need to buy, and hire who we need to hire in order to carry out the instructions of the Lord. Many ministries are limited financially, especially when they are in a small church. I believe a large part of the problem can be overcome through partnership with those who are gifted to create wealth.

To start a business owners group in your church, find a seasoned business leader that:

1. Believes in the vision of the local church.
2. Is in good relationship with the other leaders in the church.
3. Is a regular financial supporter.
4. Has credibility in the eyes of the people.

This leader (or couple) needs to understand and teach the basic theologies of the church, the vision, structures, and strategies and represent the heart of the pastors. They are managing a department on the pastor's behalf. The marketplace initiative should not be a standalone entity, but totally integrated into the ministry dynamic of the church. Business leaders need to communicate with the senior pastor about issues, strategies, or opportunities, as well as taking the initiative to stay informed about the present challenges the church is facing. If communication breaks down and the marketplace is going one way and the clergy is trying to go another, it is like a house divided against itself and it will not stand.

The second step in the development of a marketplace ministry is to help the leader (or couple) build a leadership team. During the social interactions and functions of a business owners group, natural relationships begin to form around a common vision. Vision is built around or through relationships. Out of the relationships, there will be those who catch the vision and become potential team members. Team leaders need to identify possible members, but must also get them approved by the pastor before asking them to become team members. Once again, this is due to the Freedom of Information Act.

The third step is to designate responsibility to each team member so that each one has a specific role and responsibility to carry. This is done by taking the vision and dividing it up into individual parts, then delegating those parts to individual people.

The last step is to help the individual team members build a team to carry out their task, if the task is large enough to warrant more than one person.

At every level, relationships and communication are the main focus of success. The marketplace initiative should be a reflection of everything the local church is called to be and do. This creates a church with no walls, one that is truly pastoring its city.

SIXTEEN

FINAL THOUGHTS

We spend so much time trying to get people to attend church, but let's make a strategic shift to just building churches that people want to attend. I hope this book has inspired some thoughts for you and given you some tools to be all that you can be. I have a passion and desire to help the men and women of God who are working hard in a garden that may have at this time only produced a small harvest. I want to help as much as I can, but in the end we all have to come to the realization that with the help of God, we have to create our own reality; other people will not do it for us.

The goal of any church is to facilitate the success of its members. Myself and our teams of Life Church have the same desire to facilitate your success, regardless of how you define it. It isn't our intent to build a mould and hope everyone can fit into it. Quite the opposite, really. Our goal is to provide the tools, resources, and relationships you may need in order to become whatever the Lord has created you to be.

We believe you can do small church in a big way, and big church in a small way. One is not better than the other, as long as we are doing and being what the Lord has called us to. A small town mega church is simply a small church with a big impact. Our desire is to keep the church experience personal as it grows and to release the vision from centralized governing leadership into the hands of the people. Personal ownership of the vision is the greatest motivator to keep the fire burning for the next generation.

Guard the integrity of your church. I believe the church image has taken some bad hits over the last fifty to seventy-five years, but God is all about restoration. If we will guard the integrity, He will produce the harvest. I don't want to just start churches all over the world; I want the churches that have already been started to finish strong! Don't take shortcuts or look for the program or scheme that will birth a revival or build a church without much work. Shortcuts in church growth usually work out about as well as get-rich-quick schemes. There is always lots of noise from those who claim they can do it, but I have never met one who has. Just settle in and enjoy the journey. The journey is what has value; the destination is heaven.

Success isn't measured in just numbers. It is measured by the peaceful yet purposeful intentions of the people who are enjoying the journey. There will always be tensions, differences, offences, and separations. It happened with Paul and Barnabas, and it will happen again in today's body of Christ, I'm sure. We can, however, deal with differences, offences, and troubles with a humble spirit that honours one another. There are no perfect leaders. There is nobody who knows it all. There isn't anyone who has all the gifts, and there isn't anyone who hasn't got hidden fears and failures. The goal isn't perfection, but we can be transparent. Transparency doesn't mean that I am going to go public with all of my failures or weaknesses, but it does mean that I will be real about my limitations, honest about my intentions, loyal to those who follow, and proud of all who rise above me.

A violation of integrity will cause people to not believe what you say—perhaps for many years! So keep your life and leadership as pure and simple as possible. I know the Lord wants us to teach on purity, but a pure life is as much caught as taught. As leaders, we can set the standard. We must remember, as leaders in the house of God, that the lowest standard we accept as normal will be the highest standard most of our congregation will strive to achieve. Set the standards high, but grace even higher! I don't try to hide my failures. I celebrate with humility, but I repent publically. I don't want our people to think that God has done all this in my life because I did things better than them, or that I have some special favour of God on my life that they cannot have. I want them to see how we work through failures. I don't think we do our kids any favours by protecting them from failing. If they don't learn to overcome failures, they can never achieve success. After all, failure is part of the journey to success.

The simplest way I can describe a small town mega church is found in its ability to effectively manage, market, and mobilize a vision. To do this, we need to embrace diversity and pursue intellect and gifting. We tend to think that the well-educated or successful will not come to a local church. If you surrender to the thought that the educated, charismatic, successful, rich, famous, popular, and energetic people won't get saved, that leaves you with the dumb, poor, unpopular, dull nobodies... but remember, *you* got saved. So did I!

The ultimate gauge of success will not be seen for years to come. There is no true success without successors. We are to enjoy all we are and have the greatest impact we can in our time, but it is just as important to do it in a way that passes the baton to the next generation. We need to engage the next generation now by providing them a place where young people can be taken seriously, where they can be given a chance to have input and feel that they are valued members—not just a tolerated department. We strive to give them a visible presence in all we do. This book is designed to give us tools to have a defined sense of purpose, know who our customers are, and what we have been gifted to do. With this information, our message becomes clear and our journey strategically marked out. This allows us to shout from the rooftops and clearly and confidently proclaim who we are. The goal is to make the complex as simple as possible. We tend to try to impress everyone with the depth of our knowledge, but Jesus blew us all away with the simplicity of His message.

I hope the tools in this book will help you to create an environment of inspiration for all ages. Fill them with vision, stir their passions, make room for their creativity, develop their character, and embrace change! A state of constant change may be expensive, but lack of change is definite death.

Embrace the fact that you have the highest responsibility before God. Take it very seriously and work hard, but remember that failures are part of the journey. No matter what has happened in the past, "Today is the first day of the rest of your life!"

God bless you.

PASTOR GARY

STATEMENT OF FAITH

Life Church International is an organization dedicated to leadership development, team building, church planting and growth, and effective community engagement. If you desire more information, or are interested in becoming an affiliate of Life Church International, you can contact Pastor Gary at LCI's Drayton Valley office (1-780-621-2077) or his email (garycarterinc@live.ca).

We believe:

- That Jesus is Lord of all (Philippians 2:9-11)
- In the death and resurrection of Jesus Christ (John 11:25)
- That His Word is true and it is the final authority (2 Timothy3:16)
- In the trinity of the Father, Son, and Holy Spirit (Matthew 28:19)
- In the gifts of the Holy Spirit (1 Corinthians 12)

- In the five-fold ministry of the apostle, prophet, evangelist, pastor, and teacher—for the equipping of the saints for the work of the ministry (Ephesians 4:11-16)
- In the body ministry of the church (1 Corinthians 12:12-26)
- In Spiritual warfare (Ephesians 6:12, 2 Corinthians 10:3-6)
- In the spiritual authority and mandate of the local church (Ephesians 3:10)
- In the great commission (Matthew 28:19)
- That God wishes that none should perish (John 3:16, 10:28-30)
- In the Biblical view of family and marriage (Ephesians 5:22-33, 6:1-4)
- That we can and should live an abundant life in Christ (John 10:10)
- That prayer is the foundation of all things (Luke 19:46)
- That healthy relationships are the key strength of the body of Christ (Acts 2:46-47)
- That we are created for a purpose (Jeremiah 1:5, 29:11, John 18:37)
- That woman are equal and are called to be leaders in ministry (Galatians 3:8, Acts 18: 24-26, 21:9, Romans 16:1-5, Micah 6:4)
- In the principles of tithing (Malachi 3:10, 2 Corinthians 9:6-15)

STATEMENT OF FAITH

- In the restoration and reconciliation of fallen man by grace, rather than by law and consequence (Ephesians 2:8-9, Romans 5:20, 2 Corinthians 12:9, Romans 3:20, 4:15, Acts 3:19-21, 2 Corinthians 5:18,19)
- In the practice of communion (Luke 22)
- In water baptism by full emersion (Matthew 3)

OTHER RESOURCES AND BOOKS AVAILABLE FROM PASTOR GARY

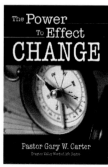

Every church has a desire to bring transformation to their city and nation. There are three necessary strategic elements to bring about lasting change. The local church must fulfill the mandate to equip the saints for the work of the ministry, be engaged in safe and yet effective spiritual warfare and mobilize the marketplace ministries. This three cord strand is not easily broken.

We have all been given many prophecies for our church or city that have not yet come to pass. The "Power to Effect Change!" will give you strategies to bring "Prophetic revelation to an Apostolic reality." This book explores the concepts of "Redemptive purpose" or the reason your church or city was birthed in the first place. It shows how to change and maintain the spiritual climate of your city through prayer and corporate team dynamics working in and through the local church. We clarify the call of a modern day apostle and package it all together into a layered anointing.

If you are a Pastor, Intercessor or Marketplace leader that is involved in city transformation this book is for you. It will give you many practical but powerful principles to help you reach your goal.

OTHER RESOURCES AND BOOKS AVAILABLE

The information Pastor Gary has recorded in this book is based on applied and proven structures and strategies used to plant and strengthen many churches. By following the concepts presented you can and will establish jurisdictional authority in the spiritual realm and bring your entire city into community alignment!

This book is designed to mobilize the body of Christ to transform cities and nations!

To order this book, visit Amazon.com or www.life-church.ca, or call 1-780-621-0277.

SEMINARS:

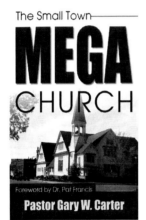

The Small Town Mega Church:

This seminar is based on the principles of the STMC book you have in your hand. It is designed to help your team identify, prepare to reach, and break through your next growth plateau. The workshop will guide you through the template to clearly define your vision and goals. You will be able to describe the atmosphere you wish to create, determine the bait to use, mark out your journey, and establish the gauges of your success. The template information that your team will create through this seminar will give you clear direction and align every department towards a common goal. This will add strength and momentum to your church.

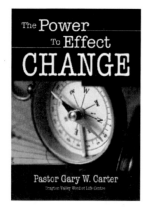

The Power to Effect Change:

This seminar is based on the principles of the PTEC book. It is designed to help those who are working on effective community engagement strategies. We explore the strength and protection produced by the three-cord strand of: the local church as the equipping centre, safe and effective spiritual warfare, and the mobilizing of marketplace ministries. This seminar is available on CD.

The Keys to the Kingdom:

Many Christians are bound up in a prison of isolation, offence, victim mentality, or poverty mindset. This is a "Breakout" seminar that will re-establish your authority and give you keys to freedom!

For more information on resource materials or seminars available, visit our website at www.life-church.ca or give our Drayton Valley office a call at 1-780-621-0277.